AN INTRODUCTION TO CHRISTIAN SPIRITUALITY

BY

STEPHEN HASKELL

Published by New Generation Publishing in 2020

Copyright © Stephen Haskell 2020

First Edition

The author asserts the moral right under the Copyright, Designs and Patents Act 1988 to be identified as the author of this work.

All Rights reserved. No part of this publication may be reproduced, stored in a retrieval system or transmitted, in any form or by any means without the prior consent of the author, nor be otherwise circulated in any form of binding or cover other than that which it is published and without a similar condition being imposed on the subsequent purchaser.

ISBN 978-1-78955-896-8

www.newgeneration-publishing.com

New Generation Publishing

FOR FELIX, ELIZA, NATALIE AND MADDY

Contents

INTRODUCTION	1
FAITH	3
HOPE	17
CHARITY	25
PRAYER	34
THE SACRAMENTS	43
CONVERSION	54
THE LATER STAGES	63
CONSCIENCE AND SIN	74

INTRODUCTION

This book sets out to be no more than the title suggests: a brief introduction to what seem to me the basic questions of Christian spirituality, together with my answers. But others will find different questions, provide different answers, and above all treat the subjects at greater length.

It is aimed at all Christians, and at any who have an interest in Christianity. Although I am a Roman Catholic, it should be free of all sectarianism. It is only in the chapter on the sacraments that different branches of the Christian church will find issues of relevance to their own particular denominations.

Readers who notice such things may have been puzzled by the fact that the word church sometimes appears in capitalised form, and sometimes not. But there is a purpose to this. When capitalising the word, I am thinking of the whole baptised community of Christians, including the early Church, though it wasn't long before different bodies forced it into division. For individual churches including my own, I have kept the word in lower case. I have tried to be as consistent as possible, but mistakes may have crept in.

The book is obviously addressed to both male and female readers. I tried at first to write it in inclusive language so that no one could think I was favouring one sex above the other. Alas, such attempts run up against the stringencies of the English language. You can either say 'he or she, his or hers' throughout, which becomes very tedious for reader and writer; or you can follow a singular noun by a plural possessive adjective: i.e. The Christian should never lose their temper, which offends my sense of grammar. Sometimes the problem can be got around by putting the original noun in the plural: i.e. Christians should never lose their temper. But this does not always suit what one is trying to say.

Most of the Biblical quotations are taken from the Catholic edition of the Revised Standard version, but occasionally I have gone to the King James Bible, whose rhythms are incomparable.

If there is one thing I should like to see taken from this book, it is that Christian lay people are just as capable of rising to the summit of spiritual life, namely union with God, as those in enclosed religious communities, but that the way for them lies through charity and not through prayer.

FAITH

What do we mean when we use the word 'faith'? I would suggest that over the years the word has come to acquire two meanings, which may fairly be described as the head and heart of Christianity.

In the first place it means the ability to believe the major facts of that religion, which are encapsulated in the Christian creeds, the Nicene Creed and the shorter Apostles' Creed. We all know how they go, and one or other of them is recited in most churches every Sunday. They attest our belief in God, the Father Almighty, who has made heaven and earth, and by extension ourselves. They couple with that belief in Jesus Christ, God's only son: that he was, in the Catholic version of the creed, consubstantial with the Father*, begotten not made, and that he is of one being or essence as the Father; that he came down from heaven and was born of the Virgin Mary; that for our sake he was crucified and genuinely died, but that this was not the final phase for him. He genuinely rose from the dead, took his rightful place in heaven, and will once more appear to judge the living and the dead and to wind up his kingdom.

We also profess our belief in the Holy Spirit, whose attributes are described, and who proceeds from the Father and the Son – this, of course, is a contentious issue between Eastern and Western churches; in one holy catholic and apostolic church; in one baptism; and of our place, and that of all the dead, in God's eternal kingdom.

So much for the content of the creeds. But, as will be seen from this very brief attempt to summarise them, they give us only the bare facts, and in some respects may be regarded as positively misleading. Take God, for instance. They rightly regard him as the supreme creator, but they give no indication that he was not himself created, and is wholly outside time. They also call him 'The Father', which is a term inherited from the Jews, and which Jesus himself used in the gospels. But the attribution of gender to God is of course a gross mistake. It is to anthropomorphise him, something we cannot help doing. He is of no gender at all, but the Jews, being a patriarchal people, could think of him in no other way, and it is this term which Jesus himself uses in the gospels; and this, so long as we remember its limitations, seems as good a reason as any to maintain the name. Nevertheless many people – and Julian of Norwich is one of them – have preferred to think of him as a mother; and this has proved particularly popular in a time like ours, when patriarchal values are on the wane. But whatever name we give him (or her) we have to remember the shortcomings of human language when dealing with one whose true nature lies totally beyond our comprehension. We do the best we can.

The same, to an even greater degree, applies when we talk of Jesus 'sitting at the right hand of God'. What we mean, of course, is that he is in his rightful place in heaven, assisting God in the redemption of creation. But for children, and even in the unconscious of some adults, this conjures up a view of two chairs balanced perilously in space – is there a third for the Holy Spirit? – and is on a par with thinking of God as an elderly man with a beard, rather akin to Father Christmas. Artists are faced with the same dilemma when trying to portray him; for if we think of him as a personal God – that is to say with the capacity to love each one of us – then the only way to portray him is to give him a human face and body. It is, as I say, the equivalent of the limitations of the human language.

One of the themes of John Robinson's book, *Honest to God*, published in 1963, was that we should no longer think of God as a being outside our world, someone 'up there'. This is a gross simplification of his work, which attempted to place God at the centre of our being; but again, perhaps unconsciously, we do tend to think of heaven up there, and hell down below. This is common to many cultures, and comes from the notion that our view out in space is unlimited, while what lies below the earth is hot, dark and dangerous. But we have to realise that concepts such as heaven and hell are spiritual realities, and that we can get a foretaste of both in our present existence. It is in any case fanciful to terrify people with the thought of physical torture immediately after death, as was done until surprisingly recently, since Christian belief is that, until the general resurrection, we have no bodies when we die. A far closer approximation to truth – and yet again, we are dealing with an incomprehensible state, though the best that human language has to offer – is that in heaven we shall fully share God's nature, while hell has been described by one of Graham Greene's characters as 'a permanent sense of loss'; he goes on to state that if we do not fully understand this, it is because we have never lost something we loved.

Something which comes closer to Jesus' own image of a place 'where their worm dieth not' is to think of it as a state of vain remorse, a constant rending of the soul over what it has done and cannot now undo. We do not know, of course, whether anyone actually goes to hell, or whether the most hardened sinner may eventually find forgiveness. All that we know is that the attempts to portray such concepts as heaven and hell run into the inevitable handicaps of the human language.

Thus the creeds offer the bare bones of Christian belief, they are, if one likes, a sort of passport which lists the essential facts of one's age, place of birth, and appearance, but misses out the most essential of all, what one is like as a human being. If all we knew about God was what we had in the creeds, it would be very hard to love him. For further knowledge we have to go to the Bible, and in particular to the New Testament.

Seeking knowledge of God solely in what we find in the Old Testament, we should be highly confused. He is by turn vindictive (to the third and fourth generation), faithful and continually renewing his covenant with Israel, but determined that they should annihilate their enemies, and ready to punish them if they do not do so (1 Sam 15), with a plan for his chosen people (as is shown, for instance, in the birth of Samuel), a little bit arbitrary, but ready to be swayed by intercession, as in the case of Abraham for inhabitants of Sodom and Gomorrah, and many times of Moses when he intercedes for the faithlessness of the people of Israel... The list is endless. It is only in the later prophets, particularly the second or third Isaiah and Hosea that we begin to learn of his tenderness, his readiness to forgive, and – a difficult step for the Israelites to take – of his desire to embrace all mankind, and not only his chosen people, in his love.

The Old Testament is, in fact, the highly anthropomorphic story of his gradual leading of the people of Israel until they were ready to embrace a Saviour (which of course, many of them, besotted by their previous history, did not). It is only in the New Testament that we begin to realise, both in the person of Jesus and in what he says, what God is really like. Jesus said both 'the Father and I are one' and 'if you have seen me you have seen the Father.' He is by turn stern and demanding, but all the time ready to forgive and full of consuming love. Two particular images stand about from Saint Matthew's gospel. In one (10:29) he says 'Are not two sparrows sold for a penny? And not one of them will fall to the ground without your Father's will ... Fear not, therefore; you are of more value than many sparrows.' And in the same passage he says that 'even the hairs of your head are all numbered.' I used to see these as mere metaphors. But now I am convinced that we should take them more literally. God's love exceeds all that we could ever know of him. It is boundless, infinite, personal to a degree that we scarcely find acceptable. It embraces all that we hate about ourselves. God can never hate; he can only love.

Jesus also said (John 3:16), 'God gave his only-begotten son so that whoever believed in him should have life eternal', and this theme is echoed in the liturgy. But 'giving' seems to imply that it was a sacrifice on God's part too, that he was giving up something, or someone, he loved, was missing him, was in fact also suffering. But can God suffer? We are inclined to think of him as above all this, as caring for us, certainly, but remaining the same whatever we do or say. Does God in fact suffer when we reject him, when he views the many injustices and torments in the world he has created? In the parable of the Prodigal Son we learn nothing of the feelings of the father while his son was away. This is a great mystery, and I do not pretend to have the answer. But we should at least consider the possibility that we are hurting God whenever we turn away from his will.

I spoke earlier of 'hating ourselves'. Maybe this is too strong a word, applicable in any case to only certain human beings. But it is undoubtedly a fact that many of us have a part of ourselves that we at least dislike and that we should like to conceal from others. This probably accounts for the fact that most of us are frightened of God: far more, certainly, than are frightened of hell.

We are constantly told that God is a loving God, full of forgiveness, certainly not ready to trip us up or to wish us to think evil of our enemies. Yet this is the way we persist in thinking of him, quite differently from the 'fear God' which we are told (Job 28:28) is the beginning of wisdom. Why this arises, and is capable of haunting even those who are well advanced in the spiritual life, is a bit of a mystery. One reason has already been suggested for it: it is really dislike of ourselves which we are convinced that God shares; and so, in this situation it is natural that we should be afraid of him. We are reluctant to confess to him all of our faults; we keep back from him something of ourselves even in prayer. And until we have learnt to deal with this, to hold nothing back, our prayer life cannot be entirely successful.

But it seems to go back further than this, to ally ourselves with our ancestors who, while worshipping the sun or moon or whatever, were also aware of the frightening direction nature could take, and were ready to attribute this to the wrath of their god. Much of religion – and this even applies to the religion which we, who like to think of ourselves as enlightened, rational folk embrace – contains elements which point to the need to placate God. We can witness such a desire even in the most cherished prayers of the Catholic faith, in the first Eucharistic prayer, for example, which three times asks God to be content with this sacrifice, as if we doubted its efficacy, or at any rate thought that one supplication would not be enough. And we can see it in that which follows the Eucharistic prayer, in which we 'dare to say' – the Latin is 'audemus', but at least the old translation had we are 'bold to say' – the Our Father, this about the prayer that Jesus taught to his disciples and told us was the correct way to address God.

We are also strongly influenced by our earliest experiences, by what are we have seen and gone through in our families. Our image of God may, for instance, depend on our experience of our own father; or, if he is absent, this may be a telling factor in how we embrace God or neglect him altogether. One school of psychoanalysis tells us that there is a period long before we have full control of our conscious selves which affects all that we say and do. More will be said of this subject when we consider why faith is given to one person and apparently denied to another.

Fear of God, however, which we are enjoined to have, is a very different thing. It recognises that he is one of a totally different scale from us, one who created us, but had no need to, one whose ways and being we can scarcely understand. So all we can do, once we come to believe in him, is to try to fulfil his commandments as adequately as we may, graciously accepting that he has made us to share his glory, though again we don't know how or why. It is this which led the Psalmist to exclaim (Psalm 8):

What is man that thou art mindful of him
And the son of man that thou dost care for him?
Yet thou hast made him little less than God,
And dost crown him with glory and honour.

Finally we come to what the creeds have to say about the Holy Spirit, the third person of what the Christian faith has taught us to call the Trinity. He is credited with being on a par with God and with inspiring the prophets. But by far the best description of his work comes in the sequence Holy Spirit, Lord of Light (translated from the 12th or 13th century *Veni, Sancte Spiritus*) which is sung or said during the Mass of Pentecost. Here he is called the consoler or comforter, the term in which Jesus often spoke of him, who 'heals our wounds, renews our strength, makes up for our dryness and purges the sense of our guilt; bends the stubborn heart and will, and guides the steps that go astray.' It is, in fact, a hymn which teaches us to love and value the Holy Spirit, something which the mere credal statements cannot do; nor indeed are they intended to.

Jesus, towards the end of his short life, had much to say about the Holy Spirit. He was coming in his (Jesus') stead, and thus, as I have said, is called the comforter. He would remind the disciples of all that Jesus had taught them, which, particularly in the long discourse which forms part of the Last Supper in St. John's Gospel when their minds were already filled with sorrow, lay beyond their memory and comprehension. They would no longer have to worry what to say when confronted with their persecutors, for the Holy Spirit would speak through their mouths; and we witness this in the brilliant way in which Paul (Acts 23) deflects the accusations against him by setting Pharisees and Sadducees against each other. In fact, the early members of the Church probably had a far more accurate sense of the Holy Spirit than we do now. The first disciples were aware of what he could do, of the power he gave them to win people over when the very existence of the Church seems a kind of miracle.

The great feast of the Holy Spirit is of course Pentecost, when he descended on the eleven remaining disciples, assembled with the Virgin Mary, and transformed them from hopeful waiting souls – had not Christ frequently appeared to them after his death they would have been frightened, scattered souls – into those who were ready to take up the role for which they had been prepared, and preach his words to the multitude. And since then the Holy Spirit has always been with the Church, ensuring its survival, saving it from doctrinal error, and gradually leading mankind into the truth. The word 'gradually' is important here, for as St John Henry Newman pointed out, the Holy Spirit's work is never done and doctrine itself is constantly developing. Those who fail to recognise this, and who would like to cling to some pristine image of the Church, for ever unchanged, for ever unchanging, are as guilty – or should that be afraid? – as those who would like it to conform to every passing whim of the multitude.

But the Holy Spirit is also in each one of us, leading us away from evil and guiding us in the right path if we are open to what it tells us to do. Jesus said that the one unforgivable sin was that against the Holy Spirit, and this deserves further discussion. But there is one other passage in the gospels which vividly describes the Spirit's work, and points out how mysterious it is. This occurs in chapter three of Saint John's gospel, when Nicodemus comes to Jesus by night. Among the other messages he receives Jesus tells him 'That which is born of the flesh is flesh, and that which is born of the Spirit is Spirit... The wind blows where it wills, and you hear the sound of it, but you do not know whence it comes or whither it goes; so is it with every one who is born of the spirit.' This is both a beautiful image and a striking example of how the Spirit works: we cannot see it, but we are constantly aware of it, and we should pray to it often – something, regrettably, which many of us fail to do.

I am not saying that the doctrinal side of faith is unimportant. Without it the Church would never have survived; without the battles of the past it would never have resolved the complicated questions surrounding Christ's humanity or the nature of the Eucharist. Some of these amounted to real battles, to inquisition, persecution, and in some cases death. Nor was the Catholic church alone in adopting such methods. It is possible now to look back, and, without condoning the violence, recognise that it belonged very much to the ages in which it occurred, and that the survival of what each side regarded as essential was at stake. Nowadays the battle is no longer between Catholic and Protestant, who have mostly learnt to bury their differences, to work harmoniously side by side, and recognise that violence was never part of their founder's creed. Meanwhile a more interesting scenario has taken their place. What are we to think of religions like Islam, which claim a large number of adherents, and which in some ways are similar to Christianity – in the emphasis they put on charity, for instance – but in other ways are totally different, in that they would regard worship of the Trinity as blasphemous and deny Jesus any part in the godhead?

So far what has been discussed is faith in its doctrinal aspects, the truth which the Church proclaims, and which it has resolved into concise clauses over the ages. But I am not at all sure that faith of this kind is sufficient to turn us into real Christians. We can believe everything that the Church believes, and fervently recite the creeds whenever we find ourselves in a sacred building, but still be lacking in charity, and in the essential quality of faith, what I have described as its heart. The word 'faithful' gives us a clue. It has little to do with belief, but it implies adherence to a person or cause which we have once taken up and must never relinquish.

The question has in part been answered by the church's treatment of the Jews. Until 1962 the Good Friday prayers, which cover all aspects of Christian and non-Christian life, prayed for the 'perfidious' Jews. This went with a long history of hostility – in some cases open persecution – towards the Jews as the instigators of Christ's death. It is true that this word 'perfidious' was to be understood in the sense of unbelieving rather than treacherous, but the latter meaning could easily be read into it, and it went with the idea that the Jews had betrayed their faith, and that their covenant with God was over.

The Second Vatican Council however, saw to a remarkable transformation in the church's attitude towards the Jews. The Good Friday prayer now prays 'for the Jewish people, first to hear the word of God, that they may continue to grow in the love of his name and in faithfulness to his covenant'. In other words, the Jews had a future, the debt Christianity owed to them was recognised, and henceforth the attempt to convert the Jews, as their only hope of salvation, was no longer to be attempted.

It is true that the Jews are a special case, something which should have been recognised long before it was, as the people who had all along been prepared by God for the advent of the Messiah; and it was their leaders, rather than the Jewish people as a whole – after all, Jesus, Mary, and all his disciples were Jews – who had hastened his death. But it does mark a way in which the Church is capable of regarding Islam.

Islam also does worship God. It is true that he is a different God from that which is worshipped in the Christian Church, but he is God none the less. God himself cannot be divided. Though people differ in their interpretation of him, he is present in the minds even of those who deny his existence but try to follow some formulation of their conscience. I am not saying that no effort should be made to enlighten – convert, if one likes – such people, but it must be done with full respect for the traditions from which they come, and with a recognition that Islam, in its true form, speaks for the conscience of a large part of the world.

Returning, however, to this meaning of faith as something which activates the minds and hearts of Christians, we find that Jesus himself demanded faith in those to whom he came to bring his message. The word is constantly mentioned in the gospels: Jesus could work no miracles in his home town because of 'their lack of faith'.

Whenever he performed a miracle of healing he asked if they believed, or said that their faith had saved them. He praised the faith of the Roman centurion as greater than any he had met among his own people (Matt 8:5), and rebuked Peter for his lack of faith as that which had condemned him almost to drown when trying to walk on the water (Matt 14:25). Indeed, he said that if only we had faith we could command a mountain to implant itself elsewhere. So what was this faith? It could hardly be the faith that we had described in the earlier part of this chapter, the doctrinal faith which, it may be said, was what mattered most to the Church until a deepening of its meaning occurred with the Second Vatican Council, since the definitions of what the Church believed about the nature of Jesus lay many centuries into the future.

No, what Jesus meant was belief in his ability to heal, which amounted to belief in himself as the chosen one sent by God; this was the first meaning of faith among Christianity's earliest adherents, belief in Jesus as the Messiah, and above all adherence to that belief. After all, said Peter (John 6:68), when many had come to doubt him, who else should we go to? 'You have the words of eternal life; and we have believed, and come to know, that you are the Holy One of God.'

But Jesus left a Church behind, so that for many people that simple sort of faith does not suffice, and has largely been superseded by faith in the Church as the divine source of knowledge and our guide in all we should say or do. If you were to ask a number of Christians, but Catholics in particular, what constituted their faith, most would reply faith in the Church. After all, that is what they have been taught from their earliest days if they were baptised as Catholics; and if they have maintained their belief, it is again to the Church that they owe it, though even practising Christians may speak of the importance of something they have read, the witness of a friend, or the fact that they are married to a Christian partner. And this is as it should be. For Jesus' last task – and, it may be said, one of the purposes for which he came – was to establish the Church on earth, which is henceforth the body which carries on his message and the medium through which we acquire our own faith.

This does not mean that the Church is always right in what it says or does. Recent events, for instance, show that its leaders are just as capable of sinning as the least of its members, that it has been responsible for much cruelty in the past, and that even in what it believes to be part of the mission entrusted to it – its treatment of Galileo, for instance, or its attribution of divine status to the *Syllabus Errorum* (1864) – it can in many instances be mistaken. Nonetheless, it is Christ's creation, his chosen method for spreading his message of truth and salvation. We can rail against it as much as we like, decry its methods, point to its misdeeds, but we will not find its substitute on earth, there is nowhere else where we can look for the truths that God has given us.

This then is the meaning of faith, in the second sense in which I am using that word. It means shedding one's own resistance if it is present, being ready to believe, acceptance, and then adherence. This last is the quality which many people find difficult. Those who have been born Catholic meet many creeds which compete for their faith; and all, cradle Catholics and converts alike, sometimes find it difficult to persevere when life goes on in the same old way, and their faith, apparently, makes no difference to the way they perceive the world. But this adherence, which we can witness in Peter's response above – there seems a kind of weariness in his words: now that we have come this far, there is no alternative to our following you – is a vital component of our faith, and more will be said of it later. For the moment it is sufficient to say that there is nothing wrong in finding our faith tedious, in wishing we did not have to go along with it – this is very much akin to the illusion that the grass is always greener on the other side of the street – in persevering because of routine. Sometimes these facts, that he may have to struggle with his faith, are hidden from the convert. I suppose it is a bit like marriage: there are long periods of routine in it which can at times obscure the delight in each other's presence that drove couples together in the first place. But wise people get over these difficulties, and realise that periods of fatigue do not mean that the marriage is over, or that one was wrong to undertake it.

There remains one final aspect of faith to be dealt with. Why do some people have it while for others it is the last thing they would embrace, and still others pass their lives in total indifference to it? The short answer is that it is a gift, it is God who implants faith into our hearts. But I have always felt that this is too easy an answer. Apart from anything else, it possibly reinforces the sense we may already have, that God is a wilful, unpredictable God, who does things in his own way and cannot be trusted. It may well be that the final ability to accept him into our lives is a gift, depends on him; but there is a good deal we can do to make his task easier, to clear the way for what he would surely like to impart.

In the first place we should be ready to listen, to shed our own prejudices, and to give Christianity a fair trial in our minds. This is less easy that it sounds, for these prejudices have been built up over periods of time; they depend, as we have already seen, on our earliest experiences, and can never, perhaps, be entirely removed.

In the second place, there are many other things which compete for our attention: our families, our jobs, and all the other factors that make up everyday life. It is hardly surprising that with all this on our minds we should scarcely find time to think about God, or that he should take a secondary place in our concerns. But it is surely part of every thinking person's make-up to want to know truth. There are many different kinds of truth: scientific, historical, ethical, and so on. But the one that really matters is what we are doing on this earth, what is our purpose, if any, why we were created.

I'm not saying that problems of this nature can all satisfactorily be solved by deep thought or even prayer. To begin with, those who already have their version of the truth are inclined to be satisfied with it. They are unlikely to want to give it up for the sake of another, which may seem to their eyes entirely mythical. But there is no real difference in this context between prayer and being ready to listen. Such people should at least be ready to examine the evidence – I do not mean Aquinas' five proofs, though these may be useful to those who think in a logical way – but the evidence that is to be found in the New Testament, primarily the gospels. Was Jesus just an ordinary sort of prophet, maybe a charlatan? Did he perform miracles, or were the evangelists totally – perhaps deliberately – mistaken in what they record? Was he really crucified? Did he rise from the dead, or is that just another of the stories his followers concocted, perhaps – and this is to lessen their guilt – an example of mass hallucination? All these are important questions, at least not summarily to be dismissed; and how were these frightened disciples transformed into those who spoke out boldly at Pentecost, and what was it about Christianity that within three centuries transformed it into the official religion of the Roman Empire?

I end this chapter not with an entreaty that all should embrace my point of view, but that they should at least show openness and honesty to what has been here described.

Note
* Many people have criticised the word 'consubstantial' as being incomprehensible to most Mass-goers. However, it is a pretty accurate translation of the Greek 'homoiousios', and the new version, 'born of the Father before all ages', is certainly preferable to the old 'eternally begotten of the Father', which seemed to imply a process of continuous generation.

HOPE

What is hope? Christian hope seems to me to be very closely linked with Christian faith: that is to say, if one did not have faith in Christ's saving mission, one would hardly have hope that one day one would be with him in heaven. But there are other aspects of hope which seem to me worth exploring.

In Shakespeare's *Richard III* Gloucester, soon to be King Richard, is wooing Anne, whose husband and father he has killed, and the following two lines of dialogue occur:

> Gloucester: But shall I live in hope?
> Anne: All men, I hope, live so.

The scene is not meant to be taken too seriously. Shakespeare is juggling with words here, and Anne, though she later yields, is fending off his advances. Nevertheless, her answer does seem to me to be saying something essential about hope. It is necessary to have hope to live. This is not necessarily Christian hope, but it is an essential part of our human existence.

Similarly, in Greek mythology, in a tale that echoes the story of Adam and Eve in the Bible, Pandora, the progenitor of the whole human race, is given a wooden box, and when she opens it, out fly all the ills to which the human race is subject: famine, disease, war, hatred etc. But last of all comes hope (the story thus has a slightly more optimistic ending than the Jewish myth). We are not told what this hope is attached to. But presumably it is something that will sustain the human race in the future, a weapon against all evils that she has previously let out.

Thus, hope does not seem to me to have to be directed towards a specific object, or even to be very closely tied to the future. It is certainly an expectation. But an expectation of what? That life will change; that whatever the future holds, it will be different from what it is now; and we experience this change through the thoughts and sensations that pass through our mind.

It is precisely this expectation, this experience of change, that vanish in the state known as clinical depression. Here one is perpetually stuck in the present. Nothing changes. There is no expectation that life will be different from one moment to the next. And for this reason it is one of the most painful conditions known to human kind.

This is perhaps a digression, but it does illustrate how ordinary hope differs from Christian hope, which in the early Church was firmly tied to the resurrection of Christ and to the expectation of his Second Coming. The first is most prominent in the speech of Peter made to the assembly on the very day of Pentecost. Jesus was the prophet foretold in the Old Testament; everything had been done with God's foreknowledge, including his death and his rising from the dead: they must now recognise him as the usher of a new era by repenting of their sins and being baptised in his name.

The resurrection was also very important to St Paul: 'If Christ has not been raised,' he says (1 Cor 15: 17) 'your faith is futile and you are still in your sins.' But he was also at pains to emphasise that in the new dispensation all were to be considered equal: 'There is neither Jew nor Greek, there is neither slave nor free, there is neither male nor female; for you are all one in Christ Jesus.' (Gal 3:28) Slaves were to go on serving their master (Eph 6:5), but henceforth they were to be considered on an equal par with them. This was very much in line with what Jesus had said, when he had forbidden his disciples to seek power for themselves (Matt 20: 20-28), and had given them an example of his own humility by washing their feet at the Last Supper. The sense of their own equality – and we know that Paul had to fight hard to see pagans recognised on the same basis as Jews in the dispensation – must have been an enormous source of hope to the early adherents. It is something perhaps that has passed from our own experience of hope, something that we are readier to take for granted.

But there is another source of hope which we associate particularly with Paul, though it was the belief of the whole Church, and this was that Christ would come again very shortly. They must live therefore in expectation of his imminent arrival. This was what he himself had foretold (Matt 24:34), and it is the basis of one of the things that Paul had to say about marriage, though it must always be understood in the context of his belief:

> I mean, brethren, the appointed time has grown very short: from now on, let those who have wives live as though they had none, and those who mourn as though they were not mourning, and those who rejoice as though they were not rejoicing, and those who buy as though they had no goods, and those who deal with the world as though they had no dealings. For the form of this world is passing away. (1 Cor 7 : 29-31)

Nowadays, of course, this expectation has vanished, though it is still to be found in a few cults that come particularly to the fore at some important turning point on earth, such as the new millennium. They also have a way of ending in disaster: witness Jim Jones' community in Guyana and the Waco community; and I often wonder at the boldness of such prophets who can predict to the very hour the time when the end of the world will come. How do they feel when such an event does not occur? And, more importantly, how do their followers feel about them? But this is by the way. The Church now wisely abides by the words spoken by Jesus just before his ascension: 'It is not for you to know times or seasons which the Father has fixed by his own authority.' (Acts 1:7)

This has not stopped the translators of the new Catholic liturgy from introducing into the creed a minor change, so minor that it may not even be noticed. Whereas before we used to say 'I look for the resurrection of the dead' – in other words, I expect it, I know that this is what the Church teaches – we now say 'I look forward to the resurrection of the dead,' which gives a completely different meaning. Both are legitimate translations of the Latin verb 'exspecto', but one wonders why the translators should have made such a change. For a start, it happens to be untrue. Though I repeat the phrase every Sunday I say the creed, I do not think of the Second Coming, let alone look forward to it*, from one week to the next; and I suspect it has passed from the thinking of most ordinary Christians.

But one thing has not changed, and that is the hope received as a result of Christ's death and resurrection: and we are reminded of this every time we attend a funeral. This is a very solemn occasion, and the care and love with which the dead person is entrusted to God, in the hope that he or she will be joined with him for ever, remind us that death is not the end, that our time on earth is only a passing state. If ever, then, we are reminded of our mortality, it is here; and it is surely not unusual if, in addition to the dead person, we allow ourselves to dwell on our own possible futures.

But, this apart, I do not believe that Christians think all that much about their own death, except, perhaps, when they are in sight of it, or when they are struck with some mortal illness. The times are past when children were exhorted before they went to sleep to dwell on the last four things, and also when Christians were ridiculed for always having their eyes fixed on a future state, to the detriment of their present lives, something which was known as 'pie in the sky when you die'. There may be Christians of this sort, but they now form a very small minority. For most, hope is rather like faith, something which influences their actions but which they do not dwell upon, something which they carry around with them but do not constantly refer to. Hope is thus perhaps best described as a state of mind rather than a conscious act.

But what of St Paul's second source of hope, the assurance that all are equal in Christ, that distinctions between men and women, slaves and free, Jew and Greek, do not apply? Here one can only say that with regard to our own country the situation is improving, but by no means perfect. It is not so long ago that Catholics were forbidden from so much as attending prayers with members of other Christian denominations. Now Catholic and Protestant have learnt to put up with each other, even to work together, in the realisation that Jesus intended it this way, that he wished his Church to be one. Women are on their way to achieving equality with men, though the Catholic church, especially in its headquarters, the Vatican, is still a very male-orientated society. Prayers for the Jews have been altered, and they are recognised as having their own covenant with God. On the other hand, the Church still struggles with homosexuality: it concedes that the orientation of gay people is no longer to be regarded as a sin, but still thinks of heterosexuality as the norm to which all should conform.

Meanwhile the Church has had to deal with a new problem, something which Paul scarcely envisaged, let alone had to tackle: that of paedophilia. It is bad enough that so many of the clergy are involved, though the numbers proportionately may not differ all that much from those found in society as a whole. But what is really horrific is the efforts that have been made by the hierarchy to hush it up, almost as if they did not know how evil it was, and as if priests were a special case to be protected at all costs, regardless of the norms of civil society.

If we pass to other countries, and to the world as a whole, remembering that this is not what St Paul was concerned with, that he was dealing only with the Church as he knew it, we find that the situation is much less hopeful. In many countries women are denied their rights,

Christians are persecuted, homosexuals subject to the death penalty, anti-Semitism is on the increase (and this applies to this country as well), Muslims are at war with each other, and regarded by some with suspicion or even hatred. It is this which persuades me that we have yet to wait a long time for the Second Coming. The world is in far too bad a state for God to think of wrapping it up.

The two sins against hope are presumption and despair. Presumption is a way of testing God. It is saying in one's own mind, 'I can do exactly what I want. God is certain to forgive me in the end. Therefore I shall be bound by no moral law.' It may thus be described as an excess of hope, or rather hope carried to such a point that it is resolved into certainty and the one guilty of it thinks that he has to do nothing to find God's mercy. Perhaps, and in the absence of finding such a person, the best examples come from works of fiction. Don Giovanni is guilty of this when, at the end of Mozart's opera, he is dragged screaming down to hell because he refuses to repent.

In the latter case, despair, the Christian is so wrapped up in his sin that he loses all hope of God's forgiveness. The classic example is that of Judas Iscariot, who went and hanged himself after his betrayal of Jesus. He is thus contrasted with Peter, who had also sinned against Jesus, who was in equal distress, but who did not allow it to destroy his hopes of forgiveness. Actually, the story of Judas is rather more complicated than it at first sight appears, for he had made efforts to repent, and it was only when the Jewish authorities refused the return of his money (Matt 27:3-4) that he hanged himself. Was it then the heinousness of his sin that appalled him, the fact that he had given over to death one who had loved him, and in whose company he had been for the last three years? Or is there another explanation still? His fellow disciples were convinced that he had been stealing from the bag intended for the poor, so this may be the case of one so much in love with money that in the end his sins caught up with him, and it was this habitual sinning which led to his incapacity for repentance. It is one of the things that we shall never know.

For a more overt example we have to turn once again to a work of fiction, this time from Shakespeare. In the play of that name he has Macbeth say, 'I am in blood / Steep'd in so far that, should I wade no more, / Returning were as tedious as go o'er.' It has always seemed to me that Shakespeare shows in this play a greater understanding of what it is deliberately to place oneself beyond the mercy of God than anyone has before or since, and it may be that this is the reason why actors are so reluctant to speak its name aloud. Suicide is the natural consequence of despair, and though Macbeth does not commit suicide, others of his characters in the same state do. Goneril, for instance, is described by her husband as 'desperate' – a word that carried far more connotations that it does now – and takes her own life.

Suicide was, until recent times, considered the ultimate sin against God, and suicides were not allowed to be buried in consecrated ground (Shakespeare once again shows this in the case of Ophelia). Although this prohibition no longer holds sway, the Catholic catechism still takes a grave view of suicide, saying that 'We should not despair of the eternal salvation of persons who have taken their own lives. By ways known to him alone, God can provide the opportunity for salutary repentance. The Church prays for persons who have taken their own lives.' It recognises that 'grave psychological disturbances, anguish or grave fear of suffering or torture can diminish the responsibility of the one committing suicide.' These words provide a let-out, but the previous ones imply that it is still to be regarded as a sin which can endanger one's immortal soul. Society's attitudes towards suicide, influenced by Christianity, have mercifully lightened, and neither suicide nor attempted suicide is now regarded as a crime.

One thing that is noticeably absent from the concept of hope as we have it today is the excitement that was present in the New Testament, when the new word of salvation was first proclaimed. Christianity has settled down since then, as is to be expected, and though the convert may feel the same sense of joy that once animated his first century counterpart, it is no longer a general feeling. Indeed it may be said that Christianity is going in the opposite direction, that it is eliminating its special quality of hope in favour of the different kind of hope given by the gradual reform of society's values. This is to be decried. It should never be forgotten that the human race was chosen for a special gift by the arrival of Jesus, and that we now have a duty to pass on the fruits of that gift as widely as possible.

Note
* It is possible that the translators did not intend this sense, but it is impossible to take it any other way.

CHARITY

What is charity? It is the greatest of the Christian virtues. St Paul says that without it we are as 'a noisy gong or clanging cymbal.'

All the same, there is something unusual about what St Paul says in his great hymn to charity in 1 Corinthians 13. He says, for instance, that without charity, giving away all that one has or offering one's body to martyrdom – two things, surely, which would be considered the height of charity – are valueless. This seems to imply that charity has nothing in common with doing at all, but is a state of being. Yet he himself refused to take payment for his evangelisation, and was tireless in collecting money for the church at Jerusalem. So how can we reconcile these two things? Clearly charity has to start somewhere, and collecting money on behalf of others – by sponsored undertakings, for instance – is as good a way as any. But that cannot be enough. The following verses (4-7) make it plain that he is talking about much more. He says that charity is patient and kind; does not insist on its own and takes no pleasure in wrong. It bears all things and endures all things. Clearly he is referring to a state of mind – or rather of being, for a state of mind implies that it is quite sufficient to think such things, whereas, on the contrary, they should be so ingrained in our souls that no other way of life seems possible.

But before proceeding further we should consider whether charity is the best translation of the Greek word, agapé, which the New Testament writers used to express the love which God has for his creation, and which we should have for him and for our neighbour. This may seem a trivial matter, but actually it is important in establishing the precise nature of the quality which Paul, and others, deem necessary for our salvation. We all, for instance, think ourselves capable of love, and would be offended if we were told we had none. If however, we are described as 'charitable', we probably think this refers to the number of worthwhile causes we support.

Both can be considered accurate translations of the slightly unusual Greek word which the writers have chosen, and which distinguishes Christian love from philia, friendship, or eros, sensual love. It is partly a question of context. The passage from 1 Corinthians is, for instance, often read out at weddings, where 'love' seems the natural translation (though most couples recognise how much is covered by the word, how, if they are to have a successful marriage, something beyond mere physical or romantic love is required). Equally in St John's first letter (4: 16) we find the statement 'God is love', and it would sound very strange indeed to alter that to 'God is charity'. Throughout this letter, which is comparable in many respects to the better known passage of St Paul, John is speaking of the way in which we should treat each other, and, having once used the word love, it seems natural that the text should continue with it to show that we are expected to treat our neighbour in the same way that God treats us.

Love, on the other hand, has been considerably cheapened by its use in pop songs, romantic literature and films: it has so many different meanings that it is hard to distinguish any definite one that suits our purpose. Woody Allen clearly considers it inadequate to express the strength of his feelings, and in one of his films alters it to 'lerve'. Plainly there was thought to be something distasteful about 'charity' to the more up to date translations which followed the King James version: it had a patronising air about it, which is why most modern translations have gone for 'love'. But it may be that it is time to reverse the situation, in order to proclaim the distinctive nature of Christian love. After all, the image of the well-off squire or Lady Bountiful distributing gifts to the deserving poor is well out of date, nor is charity confined to the giving of money. There are many charities nowadays that do a lot more than this. They are often the first in place when disaster strikes; they provide shelter for the homeless, distribute food and life-saving equipment where it is needed, and frequently at great risk to themselves go into disease-ridden areas to control infection. Charity therefore has lost the pejorative tone it once had, and, possibly in defiance of modern taste, it is the word which will be used throughout this chapter.

But to return to the main theme, the nature of charity, and the part it should play in our lives, we need to look no further than the gospel, where Jesus makes plain its importance. It is by this that we shall be saved, he says, and not by any insistence on our faith:

> Not every one who says to me, 'Lord, Lord', shall enter the kingdom of heaven ... On that day many will say to me, 'Lord, Lord, did we not prophesy in your name, and cast out demons in your name, and do many mighty works in your name?' And then will I declare to them, 'I never knew you; depart from me, you evildoers'.
> (Matt 7: 21-3)

And as if this were not enough, he makes it plainer still in the great parable at the end of Matthew 25, effectively the last of his teaching before his death. Here charity does indeed involve doing things: feeding the hungry and thirsty, welcoming strangers, visiting prisoners, all things which call for far more than money and can involve demands on our time, lead to embarrassment or humiliation, as well as being totally alien to our nature. So St Paul is not contradicting Jesus: charity does involve action, but we only become capable of what constitutes real charity, of deeds that call for effort and often personal sacrifice, when we have become transformed, when, as the beautiful hymn 'Come down, O love divine' puts it, charity has become our outward vesture, something, in other words, which totally wraps us around.

This does not mean that we are incapable of charitable acts until we have perfected ourselves, until the transformation is complete. On the contrary, it is through such acts, however small and menial they are, that we begin the process of transformation. But both Jesus and St Paul are talking about a total remaking of our natures; and for this to take place some sort of conversion, to be discussed in a later chapter, has to take place.

It is not natural to love or show charity towards our fellow human beings in the way that we do to our families. If we study once more the passage in 1 Corinthians, we find that, in addition to being kind, we are expected to be patient, self-denying and in many cases reluctant to speak about ourselves or our virtues, not given to boasting or rudeness, prepared to give way in an argument, and never insisting on our rights. This is a hard pattern of life to conform to, and it certainly cannot be done without divine help. And if we examine what Jesus says about it, he confirms that it is not something that comes to us naturally. It is natural, he says (Matt 5:46), to love those who love us, in other words to care for one's family and those closest to us, to put all one's efforts into ensuring their happiness and rights. But this is not enough. Even those who do not have any religious belief will do as much, he says, and so in order to show our commitment to charity we have to go a step further, to a level which requires unremitting effort and sacrifice as well.

Yet it is in the family that charity has to start. We learn from a very early age that we cannot always get our own way, and that we should have regard for others. As we grow older, this expands. We try, in our own interests as well as those of others, to remain on good terms with our neighbour, in this case our schoolfellows or later those at work. Admittedly, we hear of awful cases where this law of charity is constantly broken, where the parents have no love for their children, where children develop bad habits which lead them into gang warfare, where one can get one's own way by being thoroughly unpleasant to those at work, by throwing one's weight around and showing – this applies in the family as well as in the workplace – who is the true boss of this outfit. Fortunately, these cases are the exception rather than the rule, and most families, not simply Christian ones, learn that it is better to have harmony rather than division if they are to be happy themselves.

Many Christian families say grace before meals, teach their children to pray and pray with them, and make sure that they go to church on Sundays. But it must not be forgotten that children learn as much from example as from precept, so it is no use expecting them to keep up these Christian habits if they are not shown love, which often consists in respect, in learning to treat them as individuals, frequently giving way to them, and if they do not witness that love between their parents too. There is quite a tradition of books where parents, nominally Christian, ensure that their children later abandon their parents' faith purely because of the way in which they have been treated, often in the name of religion. Fortunately, there do not seem to be too many Catholic stories among such books, which include Samuel Butler's *The Way of All Flesh*, Edmund Gosse's *Father and Son*, and more recently Tara Westover's *Educated*. I say that Catholics fortunately do not often fall within these categories, but there have been plenty of horror stories of the treatment they have suffered at the hands of monks and nuns charged with their education, and the result, causing them to abandon their religion as if it were the last thing they would embrace, may have been the same.

When we try to apply what we have learnt from our families to the world at large, we may find that it is not enough. True, we are doing our best to restrain our natural impulses, which are capable of leading us to seek our own good in all circumstances. We may have learnt to regard all people as equal, so that we would certainly refrain from seeing any group, whether distinguished by colour, creed or sex, as inferior to ourselves. We would learn to restrain our temper, even under provocation. We try to treat people kindly, and do our best to avoid cheating or lying and certainly adultery. But is this so very different from the behaviour of those who have no religion at all, who would seek at all times to be courteous to those with whom they mix, who would often stop to relieve poverty in the street, who have passed beyond extending their love to those who love them in return, and who often outdo the Christian in the behaviour which they should show to others?

There is thus another degree of charity required, one which is much more painful, and may well involve giving up everything which we have previously regarded as immutable. In this it corresponds much more closely to Paul's definition in 1 Corinthians 13, which is worth reading over and over again, however well we may think we know it, because it gives a deeper definition of charity than any other which is to be found. To practise it is to realise that charity, if it is truly to transform our souls, cannot be something to be added on to our normal Christian activities, to be limited to what we think feasible, to not going further than what common sense seems to demand. True charity may not call for a change of life; it may not be apparent to other people – Thérèse of Lisieux, for instance, was considered just an ordinary nun by many when the cause of her sanctity came up, with nothing to mark her out as special – but it is what Jesus requires of us if we are to emulate him.

For this a real kind of conversion is necessary, and God is always the author of that conversion, though to the person being converted it may seem to depend on other things: a passage in the gospel, for instance, to which he has listened a hundred times without its impact being felt, a stray word in a sermon, or by simply observing one of the beggars in the street to whom he is handing a few coins.

At any rate once this conversion has taken hold he can never be what he once was; in this, I suppose, it resembles the call to the priesthood or the religious life which a person may many times have fought against, but whose demands he cannot finally resist.

Conversations, for instance, can never be the same. Where before their purpose might have been simply to pass the time, or may have had a special purpose, such as persuasion, planning, discussion or the like, they now acquire one single end, to find out what is on the other person's mind, what they really seek, and then to make them feel better about themselves. This takes into account that what we most desire, all of us, is the feeling that we are worthwhile, that we matter. Most of us have doubts about ourselves in that respect, and the greatest source of assurance is the marriage relationship, in which, hopefully, each is totally open and exposed to their partner. But still often some doubt remains: we are not wholly sure about the worth of our personality, and this, the person who has devoted himself totally to charity is designed to fulfil.

It sounds from this as if conversations can never be light-hearted, never a question of simply passing the time with another person. But this is far from being the case. Many conversations proceed at no deeper level, and are simply a process of exchanging views with a congenial companion. But in others there is something on the other person's mind, some anxiety, some want, something maybe that they are carrying over from a previous encounter, and it is one's business to tap into this – I use this word because a great deal of delicacy is involved in such encounters – one cannot simply charge in and get a simple answer – and then to supply the help that they are seeking.

It also sounds from this as if one is making one's intervention overt, as if the other person will always be aware of what one is doing, will say to himself, 'This person is out to comfort me. He is a do-gooder, I know the type', and so he learns to resist. On the contrary one's behaviour must be totally above board, with no hint that one has any other purpose but to listen. For this is what charity is about. It does not, as Paul implies, draw attention

31

to itself. It must seem the most natural thing in the world, and thus often involves suppressing what is at the bottom of one's own mind, one's own secret anxieties or wants.

Actions must be treated in the same way. They are always done for the benefit of others, never for oneself. And if this leaves one feeling vulnerable, it is no surprise. For what one had previously relied on, what seemed to be the personality with which one was born and with which one will die, is being stripped away. The convert to charity is becoming a new person, so far without wings, and therefore very much exposed to the air.

If one persists in one's efforts, if there is no backsliding, the situation gradually improves. I will not say that the fears entirely disappear, but they become manageable, cease to bother one every time one is confronted with a stranger. And it is worth remembering the words of Jesus. He did not say (Matt 5:3) 'Blessed are the poor'. What he said is 'Blessed are the poor in spirit', which is a very different thing. There are other forms of poverty, in other words, from being without money, painful though that be, and this is one of them. One is really giving up all one owns for the sake of the kingdom, and yet life remains the same: one will be wedded to the same wife or husband, still able to rejoice in any children one may have, still continue with the same employment. The only difference will lie in oneself, and only God and oneself will be aware of it.

There is another passage in the gospels (Mark 10:17) worth considering. It occurs when a young man comes to Jesus asking what he must do to inherit eternal life. He is obviously sincere in his question, unlike others, scribes or Pharisees, who asked similar questions only to trap him or catch him out. Jesus gives him the conventional answers, based on the Ten Commandments, to which he replies that he has observed all these from his youth up. Then, we are told, Jesus loved him, and he really answers his question. One thing he lacks, he says, he must sell everything he has and give to the poor, and then the kingdom of heaven will be open to him (it is worth, by the way, comparing this with the answers he gives to others, Matthew 8:19, people who are less sincere, less committed, and who are treated with nothing like the same tenderness). But this is too much for the young man. He goes away sorrowing, 'for he was a man of great possessions.' But the seed has been planted, and who knows what he will do in the future?

The sacrifice demanded of the person who takes up charity as his life's mission is likely to be of the same kind. It will be very rare, if he is a lay person, for him to be required to adopt a completely different way of life. But Jesus knew all right what he demanded of us, and it may well contrast with the life we have lived until now. For Christianity in this country, at least, makes no great demands of one. It is perfectly possible to be a Christian and yet serve Mammon, by which I mean worldly values, and not simply money. We are all imperfect, but until we apply to our own circumstances the answer given to that young man, we have not started walking in the way of perfection.

PRAYER

How much time should we devote to prayer? Probably less than is generally recommended. Prayer is not the means by which most lay people advance in the spiritual life.

So far as the spiritual life is concerned, lay people are the late starters. The pattern of spirituality for monastics was generally laid down before the time of St John of the Cross and St Teresa in the 16th century, and has never seriously been questioned. That is to say, there are three main stages – Ruth Burrows, a present day Carmelite, calls them islands – consisting of the first stage, when the monastic is still striving to come to terms with what the new life entails (John of the Cross describes this as 'the dark night of the senses'; but while there is obvious deprivation involved, the term is slightly misleading, since there is no indication that this dark night is in any sense due to the action of God).This is followed, provided the monastic has been scrupulous in prayer and in obedience to his order, by a period of contemplation, in which he is brought into direct contact with God, and which he may well think is the end of the road; this is in turn followed by darkness, which well deserves John's name of 'the dark night of the spirit', out of which the soul may emerge into full union with God.

Unfortunately, no such clear pattern exists for lay people, and this is because, until very recent times, they were not considered capable of an advanced spiritual life. Yes, they were encouraged to pray, there was no doubt about that, and are still exhorted to do so. But confusion exists as to where such prayer leads. And this is but one of the problems which prayer throws up.

The most serious of these problems, perhaps, is whether prayer actually achieves anything. Experiments have been carried out over sick people to see whether one lot, who is prayed for, gets better, as opposed to another

34

lot who is not. It is hardly surprising that such tests have proved nothing at all. To begin with, they are akin to putting God to the test. 'Show us', they are telling him, 'that you actually care, that you are going to do something in answer to our prayers.' But it can hardly be expected that God will give in to such blackmail.

This is not how prayer works at all, but it still highlights one of the main problems associated with it. Jesus told us to pray, he bade us be assiduous in our prayer (Matt 7:7), and he also encouraged us by saying (Matt 7:9-10) 'What man of you, if his son asks him for bread, will give him a stone? Or if he asks for a fish, will give him a serpent?' This looks as if we should get directly what we ask for, something reinforced by the previous guarantee, 'Ask, and it will be given you; seek and you will find.' But we know that it doesn't work like that. Very often, however earnestly we pray, and however deserving the cause for which we are praying seems in our eyes, we get nothing for our pains. Or rather we do get something. For in Luke 11:13 Jesus says, 'If you, then, who are evil, know how to give good gifts to your children, how much more will the heavenly Father give the Holy Spirit [in Matthew this is altered to 'good things'] to those who ask him!' In other words, we may not get exactly what we want, but we shall still be rewarded. And this is on a par with the frequently offered explanation that we are not praying for the right thing, or that God will give in his own good time.

I happen to believe that prayer works, that God listens without fail to our entreaties, though he may not always respond in the way we should like him to. But what if I were not to pray at all? Do my prayers for peace actually make any difference? And what of those who have no one to pray for them? Will the friendless person in purgatory stay there longer because no one is praying for him than the one who has the united prayers of family and friends? These are the sort of questions that pass through one's mind, though, as I say, they do not seriously trouble me because I have long believed in the power of prayer.

But we are constantly exhorted to pray, whenever some new crisis presents itself, be it Brexit, war in Sudan, or some natural disaster. And this is as it should be, for wherever there is nothing we can do ourselves, apart, perhaps, from contributing money, then prayer seems the only option open to us. And even those who do not regularly pray, who, if they were asked, would give a very doubtful answer about the worth of prayer, share in our feelings of helplessness and compassion, and are prominent in their generosity.

This is, however, but one sort of prayer, intercession, though it may be the one which comes most frequently to mind when we are asked to define prayer. There are, however, other kinds, and they may be summed up in the acronym which I personally have always found useful, that is to say ACTS, signifying adoration, contrition, thanksgiving and supplication (which would cover the intercession already mentioned).

Let us for the moment leave adoration aside and concentrate on the C and T letters. Of these, thanksgiving seems to me especially important, and something which we skip at our peril. It is not always easy to be thankful to God. We may be overwhelmed by burdens, or have suffered some recent catastrophe for which we cannot be thankful. But we can, even here, at least express a desire to be grateful, even if at this moment we do not feel it; for, as St Paul assures us (Romans 8:26), when we cannot pray of ourselves, the Holy Spirit intercedes for us. And conversely, when life is going well for us, we tend to forget gratitude. We accept our good fortune gratefully, but are inclined to forget who we should be grateful to. For in truth gratitude does not depend so much on the circumstances we are going through at the moment, it should be an everyday part of our spiritual life, like the virtues of faith, hope and charity.

What do we have to be grateful to God for? Well, life first of all, which is to most people a blessing, though some would disagree. Our faith, secondly, for we would hardly be praying if we did not believe in God, whether or not we belong to a church. Our health, in most cases, though we know this can go badly astray, and in old people particularly can lead to severe illness and anxiety. Our families, our friends, our jobs – some of these at least we may presume to have. But this still leaves a class of people who can see nothing whatever to thank God for, who have never been taught to be grateful, and who thus see life as a set of disasters to be overcome.

But what of those who have no hope at all, who do not know where their next meal is coming from, who see their babies with distended bellies denoting starvation? Those who are unjustly imprisoned and fear torture and possibly death? Those whose lives are blighted by constant bombing and the fear of annihilation? Compared to these our own trials become more manageable, and if they do not, if we still feel we have reason to rail against God, we can always imitate the Psalmist, who so often takes God to task for his lack of care; or, as a last resort, follow the advice given to Job and curse God. At least these are both acknowledgements of his existence.

What of contrition? A better way of looking at it would be to think in terms of what precedes it, self-examination, for contrition implies a definite sin committed, and there is no need to accuse ourselves of countless crimes of which we are not guilty, or to regard ourselves as worse than we are. Teresa of Avila regarded self-examination as a most vital part of prayer; and we should assign to it at least as much time and care as that which we take before going to confession with a priest. It is in some ways less demanding (this appears to contradict a later statement I make, in which I say that speaking a sin aloud at least reveals its true nature to us, as more or less serious than we thought). But here we are on our own, and can face ourselves, without having to use the confessional to admit what we have done or left undone. It is easy, in formal confession, to forget what we have set out to say (though this does not mean that we shall not be forgiven for it), and sometimes difficult to find words for what really troubles us. So we may fit our sins into conventional categories which we find easier to talk about. But real self-examination – and it should be real, however long it takes us – is easier in that respect, though it may reveal parts of ourselves that we would rather not know about. It is best done at the end of the day, when we have an opportunity to reflect on what has passed, and may even be done in bed, so long as we take care not to fall asleep.

If I have left adoration to the end, it is not because I consider it unimportant, but because the words for it may not arise naturally in our minds. The other three aspects of prayer cover what is closest to us. But adoration deals with God, who is far above us, on a totally different plane from our existence. It is no wonder that we find it difficult to address him. But words from the liturgy – 'Holy, holy, holy, Lord God of hosts. Heaven and earth are full of your glory. Hosanna in the highest' – can help out if we have problems, as can the Lord's Prayer, satisfyingly simple, but something which covers all our needs. Above all the Gloria which comes near the beginning of Mass says something really significant which cannot be bettered. The first four statements seem natural enough: they ask us to praise God, to bless him, to adore him, to glorify him. But then comes one which really stretches the imagination. We are asked to ***give him thanks for his great glory***. And this, surely, is something we should never have thought of by ourselves, and which seems as far as praise can go.

How long should all this take us? Not as long, possibly, as we imagine or as we are frequently told. The two important things about prayer are the sincerity and the regularity: compared to these the length is immaterial. And we may not feel like saying all of these every day, for which we need not reproach ourselves as long as we aim to cover them all on a regular basis. A constant awareness of God is what we should be aiming at, both in and outside formal prayer; if we can cultivate this, then, as I say, the length is immaterial. So we should stop tormenting ourselves with the thought that our prayer is not adequate unless we have prolonged it beyond the point where we think it should go. Far more important is the use we make of it, by trying to put into practice all that we think we have learnt from it.

These are mainly forms of vocal prayer, though I would suggest that contrition, at least, requires deep reflection on our part, which makes it akin to mental prayer. Likewise it is not necessary, when praying for others, to go through a whole list in our minds for fear of leaving someone out. The intention to pray for them is all that matters; if someone requires our special prayer then it is likely that God will remind us, or at least that we will remember at some other time of the day, and can hastily offer a prayer for them. But we should be aiming to make our prayer less and less dependent on words. Apart from all else, this increases our faith in God. We do not feel that we have constantly to placate him with the same formulas or he will fail to take note of our prayer.

There are two main forms of mental prayer. We can either adopt a type of formal meditation of the kind that religious orders such as the Jesuits and Franciscans practise and recommend. Many will find this helpful. But we can also do something slightly less rigorous, something which leaves more to our own thoughts, like reading over a passage of the Bible and reflecting deeply on its meaning for us. There is a third kind, which many people adopt, of simply trying to be in contact with God as they pray, of adoring him and listening to him, of staying with him as long as possible. This is known as contemplative prayer. But the danger is that our own thoughts intervene, and so far from praying, we can find ourselves going into a kind of daydream or fantasy. For this reason, it is only a special kind of person who is drawn to this, and it calls for us to remain in absolute stillness, ignoring, as far as possible, the thoughts which lead us astray.

For a long time, however, and particularly for those in religious orders, prayer was also seen as the way to advance in perfection and eventually come to union with God. This changed with the advent of St Thérèse of Lisieux, the true impact of whose spirituality, popular as she is, has not fully been taken in. For her method was not to perfect herself through prayer, as the two great saints of her order, Teresa and John of the Cross, had thought necessary. Indeed we know very little of her prayer life except that adoration seems to have come naturally to her; but what she did was achieve sanctity through often unseen acts of charity and through a total dedication of her life to God. As I say, her method is followed by many, but the implications of what she did have not yet been truly assessed for their impact, particularly on lay spirituality.

If then a Carmelite nun, reared in the spirit of her great predecessors, chose – this is not really the right word, since she did not choose, but seems to have evolved a method of spirituality in line with her own temperament – a new way to advance towards God, how much more should lay people, living in a totally different sphere from those for whom Teresa and John of the Cross were writing, adhere to her methods. This will be more fully discussed in a later chapter. It is sufficient here to say that, for lay people, the outside world is that in which they are called to exercise their talents, and that Thérèse of Liseux, with her insistence on charity, may be a better model for them to follow than those who looked to prayer as a means of sanctification.

For it is sanctification that we are talking about. This would have seemed natural to one in an enclosed religious order (John of the Cross, for instance, takes it for granted that those for whom he is writing would have aimed at nothing less than union with God), but in a lay person is probably seen as close to presumption or excessively ambitious. This is because the wish to be perfect is something that appears to have dropped out of the lay mind – and this despite the reminder in *Gaudium et Spes*, one of the documents of the Second Vatican Council, that it is our duty to be holy. As I say, it seems to have passed us by. And yet we are put on this earth in order to reach perfection, and this is how we prepare ourselves for the eventual meeting with God in heaven.

Prayer, for many people, is not the source of joy it is supposed to be. They prolong the period set aside for formal prayer long after they have finished all they want to say and have ceased to expect anything more from God. Why do they do this? Out of guilt, partly, because this is what they are expected to do. Others try praying, but soon give it up, again because they are expecting too much from it. They have read all the books, which warn them of the ups and downs in prayer, how one day one can feel that one has prayed successfully, another day one can be down in the dumps because nothing seems to have happened, but that this is all the product of one's own emotions and one should not be troubled by it. But when it comes to prayer, neither of these responses seems to happen. It may be that people in this category should persevere, and they would find prayer more rewarding. Or it may be that they are simply not suited to long prayer, and having fulfilled their obligation – I am thinking here of the constituents of prayer which I have labelled under the acronym ACTS – they should start looking elsewhere for God, and primarily in daily action.

There are a very few people for whom prayer is a form of escape, a way of evading what they have to face up to in the real world. So they keep on praying because they feel safe there, and can escape their responsibilities. But this, as I say, applies to a very few. And the reason most of us prolong our prayer, or feel that we are not doing it properly unless we devote a certain amount of time to it, is that we have been taught that way. What is missing in lay spirituality is the realisation that the lay person is completely different from the monk or nun, on whom most notions of prayer are based, that they are still capable of perfection, but that they must pursue it in a different way.

One of the real lessons, however, to be learnt from those who practised prayer as a means of attaining union with God, is that they all saw the spiritual life as a dynamic process in which there was a certain pattern to be followed; and the images they use in describing it reflect this. John of the Cross, for instance, talked of the ascent of Mount Carmel, for Teresa it is a garden in which the gardener does most of the work, although in the later stages it is God himself who takes over (she later refined this, in *The Interior Castle*, to a series of mansions, seven in all, through which the soul must pass before reaching its final destination of attaining union with God). Walter Hilton described it as a ladder of perfection, whereas for Ruth Burrows it is a sort of island-hopping, with each island demonstrating a stage in the soul's progress. St Paul went so far as to say that he was involved in a race in which only one could win the prize (though we know that God does not reserve his gifts for chosen athletes, but is boundless in his generosity, rewarding all who are prepared to put their all into following him).

What these writers, therefore, had in common, was the idea that life – or the spiritual life, at least – was a journey, a dynamic affair in which we should always be looking forward to the next goal. The Church has adopted much of their imagery – for instance it is common to hear of our life described as a journey, and the Church prefers to describe herself as a gathering of pilgrims rather than the pyramidical model which was once fancied. What is missing, however, from these models is the sense of urgency which the prayer-dominated groups of the past once gave them (a pilgrimage, for instance, is usually conducted at a slow pace, with all the participants kept together). So we have to recover the sense of dynamism which the spiritual writers of the past once gave us. Yes, life is a journey – there is nothing wrong with the image. But it is a journey in which progress is made, conducted through various stops or stations which may not be the same as those through which the previous generations who sought perfection through payer passed, and with a definite destination at the end. It is only when this sort of dynamism has been restored that a valid pattern of lay spirituality will emerge.

THE SACRAMENTS

Is it possible to pursue sanctity without the aid of the sacraments? Many people are forced to do so, but that does not mean that we should fail to take advantage of them when they are available.

There are seven sacraments: that, at any rate, is the position of the Orthodox and Catholic churches (though the former recognises other rites as 'lesser' sacraments and marriage, it appears, was added later).

Many of the justifications for such sacraments are either present in the gospels or may be inferred from them. Thus, Jesus himself was baptised, and the first thing the apostles did for their converts was to baptise them, which accounts for the fact that all churches consider it necessary, though the time at which it may be given varies. Likewise, it is recorded in three of the gospels, and by St Paul, who was writing before them, that Christ instituted the Eucharist at the Last Supper and wished this to be done in remembrance of him. It is these last words which have led to so much disputation, to persecution, in some cases death, at the time of the Reformation. Was this simply a memorial of his death, something, in other words, that did not require the transformation of the elements into his actual body and blood? Or, as the Catholic and Orthodox churches have always believed, was the emphasis to be put on his first words, when he says (1 Cor 11:24) 'This is my body which is for you' and 'This cup is the new covenant in my blood.'

I said that the other sacraments may be inferred from the gospels. Thus, in John 20 he appears to his disciples after his resurrection and tells them (verse 22) 'Receive the Holy Spirit. If you forgive the sins of any, they are forgiven; if you retain the sins of any, they are retained.' It is hard to take these words in any sense than as the justification for the sacrament of Penance or

Reconciliation. But, Luther apart, the reformers did so reject them, possibly influenced by the scandal of the sale of indulgences, which seemed to make forgiveness dependent on the gift of money.

Likewise, James, in his letter (5:14), says 'Is any among you sick? Let him call for the elders of the church, and let them pray over him anointing him with oil in the name of the Lord; and the prayer of faith will save the sick man, and the Lord will raise him up; and if he has committed sins, he will be forgiven.' This seems a pretty clear mandate for the Church to declare the anointing of the sick a sacrament (though till comparatively recent times at least in the west it was known as the Last Rites and reserved for those on their death bed). The position of marriage is more complex. For a long time this was performed by the marrying couple alone, without the need for the presence of a priest or any other witnesses. But the Council of Trent put a stop to that, and organised marriage as we now know it, including the many conditions which render it valid or invalid. Yet Jesus himself took a strong view on marriage, (Matt 19) decreeing it a lasting bond between a man and a woman. He showed, moreover, his approval of marriage by his attendance at Cana where he enabled the celebrations to go ahead by the transformation of water into wine. This, then, is another example of a sacrament which can be strongly inferred both by his action and his words.

We have already seen how Luther differed from the other reformers in his position on aural confession, and he once again took a separate stand on the presence of Christ in the Eucharist. Where the other reformers were prepared to admit only two sacraments, baptism and the Eucharist, for which they could find direct mandate in the gospels, they believed that the latter was a mere act of remembrance and have maintained this position to this day. Luther, however, believed that Christ was really present, though imposing certain conditions of his own; to this day the Lutherans have followed suit, rendering much easier an accommodation with them than it is with the other Protestant churches.

The position of the Anglican church is an interesting one. In 1563, still under the influence of Cranmer, it adopted the reformers' position that there were only two sacraments, and issued the Thirty-nine Articles which stated that 'Transubstantiation (or the change of the substance of Bread and Wine) in the Supper of the Lord, cannot be proved by Holy Writ; but is repugnant to the plain words of Scripture, overthroweth the nature of a Sacrament, and hath given occasion to many superstitions.' This remains the official position of the Church of England, but is held only by its evangelical wing. It is fair to say that Anglican practice, though never clearly defined, corresponds largely to that held by the Catholic and Orthodox churches. Thus marriage, for which the presence of a priest and two witnesses are required, and in which the couple swear eternal fidelity, is to all intents and purposes identical to that practised in the Catholic church. Likewise the ARCIC discussions between the Anglican and Catholic churches were able to say that there was no essential difference between them about the nature of the Eucharist; and certainly when I, as an Anglican, was confirmed by the bishop of Ely in Ely Cathedral, it would never have occurred to me to doubt that this was in reality a sacrament. Aural confession, though never officially a sacrament, is widely available in the Anglican church, which has always put practice before principle, thus maintaining its structure as a broad church, while reluctant to be tied down too firmly by precept.

This chapter, however, is concerned mainly with the practice of the Roman Catholic church, which holds, as I have said, that there are seven sacraments, these being Baptism, Confirmation, the Eucharist, Penance or Reconciliation, Anointing of the sick, Holy orders and Matrimony. Of these it may be said that baptism has a special status, since it links us with churches everywhere, and may be said to be what it is that makes us Christian. It admits the recipient into membership of the Christian Church, and can never be repeated (though conditional baptism is sometimes given when there is doubt about the first) or repudiated. It can, at necessity, be carried out by a lay person, so long as it is done in the name of the Father, the Son and the Holy Spirit, thus strictly obeying the last charge given by Jesus to his disciples (Matthew 28:19). It is the beginning of a new life, which releases the recipient from all the sins of the past, including the guilt of original sin, and was once considered so essential that babies who died before baptism were not admitted into heaven, but had to be content with a state called limbo, though fortunately this has now been abolished.

Obviously the baby, where we are talking of infant baptism, cannot act on its own, and the parents and godparents are making promises on its behalf. But the child is the true recipient of that sacrament, and will have the choice, when it grows up, of living up to those promises, ignoring them, or repudiating them altogether (though it cannot, as I say, repudiate the mere fact that it has been baptised). And here it is necessary to say what a sacrament is. The Catholic church, in common with many other churches, defines it as 'a visible sign of an inward grace'. Thus there are always two parts to a sacrament: what the priest or deacon, or in the case of baptism a lay person may do – marriage is slightly different and will be discussed in due course – in this case pouring water over the child in the name of the three persons of the Trinity; and the grace which is conferred upon the child. The same holds true of all the sacraments: there is always an outward sign, which has the merit of assuring the recipient that the sacrament has been well and truly received; though for the grace to be truly efficacious the person receiving it must do his best to co-operate with it.

The sacraments are not thus magic. Though valid, if properly administered, whatever the spiritual state of the one who gives them, they do depend to a large extent on our working with them. It is perfectly possible, as St Paul said (1 Cor 11:27) to receive Holy Communion unworthily, in other words when guilty of a gross sin. But it is also possible to receive it casually, without a due regard for what it is, without gratitude, and without any wish to help it make one a better Christian. There must likewise be a firm purpose of amendment when we go to confession, and marriage is actually invalid if one of the partners, for instance, has made up their mind not to have children.

Marriage, in fact, was not officially declared a sacrament until the Council of Verona in 1184, regardless of the evidence in its favour, already noted, present in the gospels. This was probably because of the high regard placed on virginity in the early Church: it was, in fact, considered superior to marriage, an opinion often mistakenly attributed to St Paul, who, in expectation of an immediate Second Coming, counselled against undertaking marriage, but was otherwise content that couples should remain as they were. Moreover his words in Ephesians 5 show in what a high regard he held marriage. It took Augustine, who proved a major influence in formulating Catholic views on sex and marriage, to point out that if everybody embraced virginity the world would very quickly come to an end. But even after the Council of Trent, which did its best to regulate marriage, and which formulated many of the doctrines by which we live today, marriage practice remained rather a haphazard affair, often arranged solely by the parties themselves, and continuing at times to be celebrated somewhat irregularly.

Grace is not confined to the sacraments, as I implied in my answer at the start of this chapter. If it were, those belonging to different churches would be at a distinct disadvantage. It is certainly possible to hold that those who celebrate the Lord's Supper without believing that the bread and wine they receive are truly the Body and Blood of Christ are given grace in the same way that Catholics are; or is God condemning them because they were brought up in that church, or because it seemed to offer a better version of the truth than the Catholic? These things are impossible to know, which is why we should keep an open mind about them, and not go about condemning those who do not belong to our church, however firmly we may believe in our hearts that it is the one to which we are all meant to belong. Grace is received whenever we do a good action, whenever we sincerely pray, whenever we resist temptation. It is just that the sacraments confer grace in a special visible way, and are intended to mark every phase of a Christian's life, from the baby, 'mewling and puking in his mother's arms', to the adult sick or in danger of death.

The two sacraments which we celebrate most often, and of which we are most in need, are the Eucharist and Reconciliation. Something has already been said about the latter, but it is worth re-emphasising that we have to be honest in our approach to it, and that what troubles us most may not always correspond to what comes high on the church's list of sins. I remember in this regard, when I was writing a dissertation on confession for my MA at Heythrop College, interviewing an American priest – his nationality may not be strictly relevant to this story, though it should be taken into account – who told me of a time when he had heard the confession of a woman who had admitted to the sin of being angry with her partner. He (the priest) became in a state of high dudgeon as he told me this story, and I took its point to be that the woman had confessed to the sin of anger, which I consider to be one of the besetting sins of our time. But no, what he was in such a state about was the use of the word partner, the fact that she was in an illicit sexual liaison, and that many so-called Christians were likewise illegally united. Now it is true that her state was a sin, and that she should have been aware of it; but was she not being honest in confessing something that mattered to her so much as anger? The Catholic church, at least until present times, has always been inclined to regard the sins of the flesh with particular severity, whereas it is surely those of the spirit – such as anger, bitterness or envy – which deface us most.

For most Catholics the highlight of their week is attendance at Mass on Sundays. But there is no reason why they should not take Holy Communion more often. Most churches offer a daily Mass, while in big cities there is usually one which celebrates it at the lunch hour, though it may be asking too much of workers to give up their short lunch break and attend.

But this was not always the case. At first the Eucharist was not separated from the communal meal which most gatherings of Christians celebrated, and to which each participant brought his own contribution which was shared out among the others; it is to the disorder at this meal that St Paul (1 Cor 11:21) is referring. The Eucharist, however, soon became separated from this feast, and in the early Church was celebrated at least weekly, and sometimes daily. In the Middle Ages, however, Holy Communion began to be received less and less often, and even among religious orders frequency of Communion was celebrated as seldom as six times a year. Church Councils, most notably the Council of Trent, ruled that Catholics were obliged to receive it at least once a year, and this applies to the present day. In spite of these rulings, the reception of Holy Communion continued to be infrequent – Thérèse of Lisieux, for instance, was overjoyed when she was given permission to receive it once a day – and it wasn't until the time of Pope St Pius X, and with his encouragement, that weekly Communion became the norm.

Even so many Catholics themselves put restrictions on how often they can receive. Anybody of my generation, for instance, can remember the crowded benches outside confessionals on Saturday evenings. Had such people committed mortal sins which would prevent them receiving Communion the next day, or were they simply afraid, in awe of the sacrament in which they were due to take part? Nowadays the queues waiting for their confession to be heard have all but disappeared, the numbers attending Mass have themselves diminished, but almost everyone, except for young children and those who are not yet Catholic, receives. Holy Communion, in fact, is not seen as something of which only the holy can partake, but as something necessary, something which aids us in our own efforts to lead holy lives.

Although, as I say, grace is not confined to the sacraments, it would be very foolish, indeed wrong, for those who have access to them, to neglect them. They were instituted for the benefit of Christians and each of them is adapted to some major stage in their life. Thus baptism, which seems to me of particular importance, gives admission to the Church and cannot be repeated. Confirmation is especially linked with the Holy Spirit and ensures that the recipients, now at a stage where they are considered able to make the choice of whether they wish to continue as members of the Church, are strengthened (for that is the root of the Latin word from which confirmation is derived) by the gifts of the Holy Spirit (in the Catholic church, confirmation coincides with the onset of puberty, though in adults it is given at the same time as baptism, and in some churches the two are always combined). Marriage and Holy orders are obviously special cases for those called to that estate, though again they are designed to provide the graces needed for each of those situations. Holy orders will help the priest to fulfil his obligations, and hopefully, so far as the Catholic church is concerned, to be faithful to his vow of celibacy, while in Matrimony, the only one in which the participants actually administer the sacrament to each other, husband and wife, as we have seen, swear eternal fidelity and are given help both in that and in the raising of their children. Anointing the sick speaks for itself: it may be performed any number of times and is not confined to those at death's door, gives them strength to endure their sufferings, and in some cases may bring about relief from the sufferings themselves.

The rules governing who may or may not receive Holy Communion are complicated because reception is seen as a sign of unity, and those who are not in communion with the Catholic church are thus barred. This particularly affects those in mixed marriages, where one partner is Catholic and the other a member of some other church. At one time such marriages were strictly discouraged, and the non-Catholic partner had to give a written undertaking that any child born of the union would be brought up Catholic. Although such a ruling no longer stands, permission still has to be sought for such marriages, and the fact that the couple cannot fully take part in the Mass together is often a source of great distress to both partners, and can be detrimental to their marriage. The present Pope Francis is well aware of this, and has made it possible for the rules regarding second marriages, where the original union has broken down, and the Catholic has taken a new partner, to be looked at again. This had in fact previously been the case under what was called the 'internal forum', where, provided restitution had been done and there was no risk of scandal affecting the rest of the congregation, the priest could readmit the remarried Catholic to Holy Communion. Thus, though the matter is in the hands of the bishop – so that customs may vary from diocese to diocese – we are in effect back to the situation which prevailed until Pope St John Paul II put a stop to the internal forum.

But the Eucharist and Reconciliation are sacraments which we need to repeat over and over again. Conscience obviously plays a large part in how often we should make use of the latter, and it is impossible to give firm rules for this, though recommendations may certainly play a part. It is up to each individual, in the light of the teaching he has received, and what he thinks for himself, to decide: all that can be said with certainty is that anything one suspects of being a mortal sin should be confessed at once. The Catholic catechism says that without being strictly necessary, confession of everyday faults (venial sins) is nevertheless strongly recommended by the Church, and perhaps I am laying myself open to criticism by saying that it should also depend on where one stands on the spiritual ladder.

This leaves the Eucharist, which also gives us the opportunity of privately owning up to our minor sins, and by which they are forgiven, and which brings us into close contact with God. Indeed it is the most intimate sacrament in that respect, and we should never forget that it is Jesus whom we are worshipping when the priest has changed the bread and wine into his body and blood. It does not matter how often we partake of this sacrament. It always does us good when approached in the right way, and is really as good a reason as any why membership of a church is a vital ingredient of our spiritual lives.

However, the churches, as we know, are divided, and may not agree on the meaning of this sacrament or on any of the others we have discussed. Roman Catholics pride themselves on their faith and regard their church as being in all essences that for which Jesus Christ provided when he gave Peter the keys of heaven and hell. At the same time they may well know others, people belonging to another church or to none at all, who equal them and their acquaintances, or even surpass them, in holiness. So how can this be? Does it suggest that membership of a church is not so important after all? Or could it mean that some Catholics are so satisfied with their faith that they do not think any special effort is needed, that finding themselves in the right church is all that is required?

Membership of a church can involve one in activities which are not entirely to one's liking. To begin with, there is the necessity to attend church services at least once a week. This can be a source of joy, but there are also times when one would much rather stay in bed. There are also occasions where one gets involved in church activities. One may be called upon to clean the church, to take responsibility for administrative arrangements, and above all to obey the church's moral code, which puts a severe ban on lying, cheating, and so on, and also aims to regulate one's sexual life. One is, in fact, giving up a certain amount of freedom, which is the case when one joins any organisation.

Against all this, however, is the fact that one is in a community, and that it was through a community that Christ intended people to be saved. In other words, though not listed as such, the Church may be the biggest sacrament of all. This giving up of one's freedom is in part a myth. Would one really be drawn into a wild life, stealing from one's employers, having affairs with other people's wives, getting into drugs, doing, in fact, all sorts of things of which the Church disapproves, if not condemns, without its authority? Or would conscience act as a guardian, that which so often stops people from doing bad deeds, whether or not they are Christian? Likewise, people often say, 'I like to worship God through nature, through solitary walks on the hills, where I find myself much more attuned with him than in the stuffy atmosphere of a church.' Well, let them. There is nothing to prevent both. But we have to face the fact that Jesus Christ did not proclaim his mission solely to the individual but to the community at large. It is through this community that one finds the strength to endure when the going gets tough. One shares in the community, benefits from its prayers, comes to find one's own individuality through church worship, where a solitary spiritual life might engender selfishness or the belief that one was better than other people. There are plenty of other arguments to be raised, such as that the church provides remedies if one is drawn to sin; but the dominant factor is that Jesus intended it this way. One cannot read the gospels, and particularly their closing chapters, without realising that he entrusted his disciples with a mission, and that mission did not end with his death. We are still heirs to that mission, whether we like it or not, potential Christians, if we are not so already.

CONVERSION

Is conversion a dirty word in Catholic thought? How could it be when every year, on January 25th, we celebrate the conversion of St Paul? Moreover, Jesus gave the eleven instructions to make disciples of all nations. But we should remember that the word has different meanings for different Christians.

Conversion means change, and we witness what this entails in the very first chapters of the New Testament when John is preaching to the Jews beside the river Jordan. John knew that he was not the Messiah; he was preparing the way for someone worthier than him, someone of whom he stood in awe. His baptism, therefore – and we have Paul's word for it (Acts 19:4) – could not confer on those who received it the full benefits of Christ's baptism (though Christ himself never baptised, his disciples were commanded to do so in the name of the Father, the Son, and the Holy Spirit), which included a remission of the guilt of original sin, a total washing away of any sins they had committed, and full membership of the Christian communion. Paul, therefore, had no hesitation in re-baptising those whom he had thus found and who were ignorant of the new dispensation.

John's demands were severely practical (one sometimes wishes that repentance were that simple). Those with resources were to share them with those who had none; tax collectors were to be honest, rather than extortionate, in their work; soldiers were to refrain from violence and to be content with their pay. What strikes one about the scene, described in Luke 3:10-15, is the wide variety of people who came to him – the soldiers presumably were Roman – this also makes what happened particularly moving, that they came to him in such large numbers, there was no sign of dissent. This occurred later, among the Jewish hierarchy (Matthew 23). The people were hungry for what John came to bring, and though his life-style was harsh, and his end particularly cruel, this may have made his task easier.

This is in marked contrast with what his Old Testament predecessors had to contend with. For the Jewish people were constantly backsliding, worshipping strange gods, and in general disobeying the commands which God had established through so many covenants with their forefathers. Nor was the prophets' task made easier by the fact that they had to prepare the people for exile or speak to them in exile and tell them that this was in direct retribution for their sins (Jeremiah is one who constantly bemoans the fact that he has been saddled with this task, and of the dangers and setbacks which it brings him). Even when the Jews were brought back from exile the prophets' task was not over. There is a scene described in Nehemiah 8 where the people spend the whole morning listening to Ezra reading the book of the Law – this was probably Deuteronomy, though the chronology here is rather muddled, since Ezra did not return with the main body of Jewish exiles in 539 B.C. – once more swear allegiance to God and are sent on their way rejoicing. But this is by no means the end of the story. The Jews were a wayward people, constantly falling into sin and having to be recalled to their roots. But if there is one lesson to be learnt from the Old Testament, it is of God's constancy, his readiness to forgive, and that he never abandoned his chosen people.

These are examples of communal conversion. But what of individual conversion? And here we come up against the different ways in which separate branches of the Christian Church regard the experience. For those of a Catholic turn of mind – and I am including here the Orthodox, the Anglicans, and many of the Protestant churches – the process is an ongoing one. Newman famously said 'To live is to change, and to change often is to become more perfect.' Moreover, many of these churches have the benefit of individual confession to a priest, which is certainly a help in the process of conversion. We witness this in the annual experience of New Year resolutions. How many of these get broken within the first month? It is always easier to stick to a resolution once it has been spoken aloud to another person.

For many evangelicals, however, conversion is a one-off experience, which is why I asked the question at the beginning of this chapter; the convert is immediately aware of some change that has come over his life, of a special grace that has been given. His previous sins have been forgiven, and in many cases he has the assurance of salvation, for he has given himself over to Christ; this is regardless of the fact whether he has previously been baptised or not. We have seen what happens at the preaching ceremonies of Billy Graham and others. Those who have felt the call are invited to come up, they profess that they have been remade in Christ's name, and are thus regarded as saved. But I am not at all sure what happens if they lapse from the grace which they have been given. Can they be reconverted? Will the assurance of salvation always remain? I am suspicious of a conversion which depends on emotion alone, and in which the advent of a special message from God is received. For a start I have never gone through such an experience myself, and though that may be taken as a sign of my own inadequacies, it also points to the fact that those who have not received the experience may come to doubt the reality of their conversion. One should not be dependent, in fact, on experience alone, which easily wears off and may leave the convert disillusioned. And secondly, I know what a wayward thing emotion is, how it can play with one, how it can be up one moment and down the next. It is very much subservient to what one wants or expects. So l prefer a soberer type of Christianity – I have chosen the word deliberately, for I expect it will be regarded disparagingly by many of my evangelical fellows – one that depends less on emotion and more on rational thought.

It is true that there are certain dramatic experiences in which the convert goes through an extreme change and can point to the exact moment in which grace is given, and in which he has chosen – or been compelled – to reform his life. The most famous of these, already referred to, is that of St Paul. He had always been a sworn enemy of Christian converts and was on his way to Damascus to arrest them when he was suddenly struck blind and heard a voice from heaven asking why he was persecuting Christ himself. The scene is dramatically depicted by Caravaggio in painting. From that moment his life changed, and he became probably the greatest evangelist the Christian Church has ever known, among other things opening it up to non-Jews.

Another example is that of St Augustine. He had led a licentious youth and flirted with many heretical sects. One day he heard the voice of a child telling him to pick up a book and read. The first passage he came to was a page from St Paul's letter to the Romans in which he says (chapter 13) 'Let us conduct ourselves not in carousing and drunkenness, not in sexual excess and lust, not in quarrelling and jealousy. Rather, put on the Lord Jesus Christ, and make no provision for the desires of the flesh'. From that moment his life was changed. He combated heresy, became a major influence on Christian thought, and incidentally wrote the first, and compelling, spiritual autobiography. It may be inferred that both of these were wrestling with some inner torment, in Paul's case, perhaps, the result of witnessing Stephen's death, and so the moment of conversion, though sudden, was but the culmination of some inner struggle.

Finally, we may turn to Bunyan who was already a Puritan and therefore well prepared for the moment of grace. He has written one of the classics of Christian literature, *The Pilgrim's Progress*. But what marks that classic above all is the urgency with which Christian seeks his salvation, so much so that he leaves behind his wife and children, and the former, Christiana, only joins him to become saved herself in the second part of the work.

I suppose that conversion may be said to begin with baptism. The baptised infant is plainly not able to make promises on his or her behalf. But the godparents affirm that they will do their best to see that the child is brought up as a Christian and renounces evil (which is one reason why being a godparent should never be regarded as purely a social affair). But as the child grows up they will have plenty of opportunities to commit themselves or otherwise to the faith (and it must not be forgotten that many of these opportunities will occur in the teenage years, when the young persons' instinct is to turn against their parents and pursue their own path). The first of these occasions will probably come at confirmation when children will have to decide whether they wish to continue as Christians in the way their parents and godparents have chosen for them. But such occasions will occur all along life. At any time, they will have to decide whether they wish to plunge deeper into the faith, or abandon it altogether, and the sacrament of Reconciliation is there to help them make the choice. For conversion, far from being a one-time thing, is something that proceeds through life, and whenever one comes to this sacrament one is, in effect, asking to lead a new life, and that is why a genuine purpose of amendment is so important.

The person who chooses baptism as an adult is in a different situation, however. I myself was such a one. I decided when I was about twenty-two that I wished to be a Christian, having been brought up in no religion, though never doubting the claims of the Christian faith. I turned to Anglicanism, and three years later became a Roman Catholic. But at no stage do I remember a dramatic moment of conversion. The first of these occasions was a more or less leisurely affair: that is to say, I had had plenty of time to consider the matter, and though I converted with solemnity, that is to say with every intention of keeping to the faith and being as good a Christian as I could be, the feeling at the end was no different, really, than from that which one experiences when one has made the decision to buy a new house or enter a new profession.

The decision to become a Catholic, however, was very different. Though intellectually convinced, largely through the agency of a friend, that this was the correct thing to do, I remember all along being assailed by doubts, and in particular wondering whether this was the work of the devil to lead me astray. But when it was finally done, I experienced nothing but relief at the finality of the process. On neither occasion did I experience sudden enlightenment or awareness of grace of the kind which many evangelicals regard as necessary.

It should be said, however, that latterly the Roman Catholic church has begun preaching in a way that corresponds much more closely to the way in which evangelicals think and express themselves. For instance when I first became a Catholic, the emphasis was much more on abiding by the church's rules and being faithful to Rome (which meant, incidentally, that criticism of the Pope was never heard, and his word was considered sacrosanct even when he was not speaking infallibly). But now one hears much more about deepening one's relationship with God and remaining close to Jesus. So it may be that the different wings of the Christian Church are not so far apart as one once thought, except in this matter of what is experienced at the time of conversion.

But the business of conversion is never complete. There is always something more one can do, some other way in which one can improve one's service of God. And this is where the sacrament of Reconciliation comes in, for those who are lucky enough to have it. Of course, God will forgive sins whatever the circumstances. A sincere wish for amendment will earn his forgiveness whether or not one goes to formal confession with a priest. But for the reason I have given above, Reconciliation is helpful. Confessing one's sins aloud will give one more insight into them – one frequently feels guilty over things which have no right to be called sins, and vice versa – and a resolution, spoken in this way, is harder to abandon and thus stands a better chance of being kept.

Listening to the advice of a priest is also useful, particularly at the start of the spiritual life, when the convert is relatively fresh to it. Even if what the priest says is not especially helpful, if it reveals nothing that one could not have thought out for oneself – for priests are not depth psychologists, and cannot be expected to give fresh and meaningful advice to every penitent – simply being in touch with what the Church thinks is bound to be beneficial. Regular confession for a recently converted Christian will get him used to the Church's ways, will teach him what is or not is not a sin, and how the Church regards it.

The situation changes, however, as one advances in the spiritual life – I am speaking here of those who are seeking perfection, who have adopted, in other words, the way of life which I advocated at the end of the chapter on charity. For such people – and this applies particularly to those of a tender conscience – the need to trust God seems to me at least as important as looking for comfort in the confessional. Even if this induces a real state of anxiety, the natural result of breaking a habit and weaning oneself of that comfort, one should persist, and realise that there is much one can do oneself to rectify the bad habits into which one may have fallen, such as failing to say one's prayers regularly or never refusing oneself the extra bar of chocolate. It should be made clear that I am not advocating a total dereliction of the sacrament of Reconciliation, which obviously has an important part to play in the process of conversion. I am simply saying that circumstances may arise when one should leave all that behind and concentrate wholly on one's relationship with God. In such circumstances, learning to rely on his mercy may seem more important than anything one can gain from the confessional.

This brings one to the question of children's confession, which should in all cases precede First

Communion. Pope St Pius X established that this should take place when children are seven or eight, as opposed to the age previously adopted, which was considerably later. But it seems to me doubtful whether children of this age can properly understand what sin is. They are more likely to parrot whatever they have been told – and this is not to deny the excellent merits of their teachers – and very often, when they come to later confessions, they are compelled to invent sins because they have none of their own to confess.

Since First Communion must be preceded by confession, there is therefore a case for saying that both should occur later, when the child is, say, ten or eleven (it is worth stating, in this context, that the age of criminal responsibility in this country, when the child may be said to have fully developed his or her moral conscience, is ten, and that it is later in quite a few countries). As well as giving the child a better understanding of what is involved in confession, and thus preparing them for how to deal with it when they are older, it would also help them better to appreciate what is involved in the celebration of the Eucharist, in which they are preparing to participate fully for the first time. Confirmation could still follow two or three years later, when the child is thirteen or fourteen. I realise that this would mean reversing the changes which Pius X brought in, and it is unlikely to happen today or even tomorrow. But it should at least be thought about.

Finally, there is another kind of conversion, deeper than anything I have so far discussed in this chapter, and which is more fully dealt with in the chapter on charity. I said there that God was always the author of this kind of conversion, but that is not a reason why one should not prepare oneself for it and desire it. To that extent it is like faith which is a gift from God, but which one can pray for and desire. The only thing about a prayer of this sort, a prayer to give oneself up wholly to the path of charity, is that one does not quite know what one is letting oneself in for and it is natural that one should feel anxious about it.

For God will grant the prayer, even if it is hesitant at first, provided one repeats it often enough, and with growing conviction. But what will happen at the end is for him to decide. It may, as I say, land one with a calling to the priesthood or the religious life; it may involve a total change of circumstance and some danger, as happened in the life of Charles de Foucauld; or it may, as I have already suggested, involve no change in one's outer way of life but a great change of heart.

There is conflicting advice from Jesus about this. On the one hand, (Luke 14:28) he advocates careful thought before one takes a decision of this sort, though he follows this by saying that it is a decision incumbent upon all. On the other, (Matthew 8:20) as we have seen, he has very little time for those who make empty promises to follow him, but then request a delay, because they have more important things on their minds.

But perhaps, if we do not feel ourselves capable of this kind of conversion, if we are fearful of what lies at the end of it, we should at least give it some thought. Nothing would be more painful than to go to one's death thinking, 'I might have done more. I might have followed the path of perfection.' And why is it that more people do not take this decisive step, or at least consider it? It may be that they do not know the riches that lie on the other side, the blessings that accrue to those who have given up in a spiritual sense all that they possess on earth, and looked to God solely for their reward. It may be that the Church could do more in its instruction, should teach us that Jesus' command to be perfect is not something that we dismiss as far-fetched, as something we should do if only we were capable of it, but a command addressed to us all. And the rewards which follow will be discussed in the following chapter.

THE LATER STAGES

Can the layperson attain the summit of the spiritual life? Undoubtedly, though it will be by a different method from the contemplative.

In the past, as we have seen, perfection was reserved for a chosen few, and the normal way to achieve it was through an enclosed convent or monastery. There the aspirant would have been advised to devote himself to prayer, whose pathways had been well laid out by such saints as Teresa of Avila and John of the Cross. But in the present age has come a revolution: that is to say, the lay status has come into its own, and it has been realised, almost for the first time, that lay people are on a par with those called to the religious life and vastly outnumber them. So the question arises, what is to be done about them? Are they still to be considered as inferior citizens, or can they hope for spiritual rewards on earth? For that, after all, is what we find when we read about the religious life: such people are gifted, if they progress that far, with glimpses of God in this life. In fact more than glimpses. Teresa, though she may have been an exceptional case, underwent constant and dramatic spiritual experiences – she was even credited with levitation – some of which can no doubt be attributed to the vicissitudes of her temperament. And John of the Cross certainly expected the people for whom he was writing to set their sights on nothing less than union with God. This is what makes him such an austere writer, with a special appeal to those of the all or nothing brigade. One of the phrases which he constantly used, the dark night of the soul, has even found its way into ordinary language, and is now employed to describe any crisis, spiritual or not, which can in certain cases lead to despair.

Let us for a moment consider life in an enclosed community of this sort and compare it with the world as we know it. The first thing that strikes one is that much more time would have been devoted, indeed required, by the rules of the order, to prayer; and it is those who found they had no gift for prayer, like Karen Armstrong in the present era, who – though they may have had other reasons of their own – were forced to leave their order. Indeed, we may wonder at the fortitude of those who spent many hours in solitary prayer, as well as attending the various canonical hours of the Church, and, most importantly, the communal Mass. They did not talk much: one hour a day might be reserved for recreation. But for the most part they were left alone with their thoughts, and it is unsurprising that these should be concentrated on their spiritual state, should give rise to ecstasy – I am using this word in its modern, untechnical sense to denote a state of great joy when God was present – and something near despair when he was absent.

The second main difference between those who entered the religious life and those who remain outside it is that the former gave up their will. They took certain vows of poverty, chastity and obedience, the latter including obedience to a superior whose rule might or might not be enlightened – and we can read of many who were not – and to a community with a very ordered way of life. Their area of choice was thus severely limited, and it is this perhaps, in particular, which distinguishes them from people in the lay life.

Let us turn now to the other side of the equation, the lay people. The first thing that strikes one is that they have complete use of their will, their intelligence, their emotions and their imagination, something which is not given to those in enclosed communities. Indeed, without these they would be helpless; for modern life in particular demands taking all kinds of decisions, facing all kinds of situations, which often change so rapidly that there is no time to adapt between one and the next. Obviously these wills, imaginations and the rest require training: they cannot be used indiscriminately, and this is what I mean when I said that the Christian life is never entirely natural, that training begins in infancy and is carried on for the whole of our lives. But compared to the monastic we are free. And it would be surprising indeed if that were not reflected in our spiritual lives.

Rather, then, than trying to know God through prayer, it is important that we should seek him in other ways which truly reflect our condition and bring us in close contact with the world about us; and it is likely then that our prayer life will suffer – or more accurately that we will imagine it suffering – as a result. We shall certainly not be able to spend as long on it. Even if we should like to, there will be other things on our mind, like getting the children ready for school, and in some cases patching up a quarrel with our husband or wife which should certainly be seen to before we set off for the day. Then will come the bus, or tube, or train: inevitably crowded, and not exactly a place for prayer (though it is often convenient for saying the rosary). After this will come work; and so the day passes. There may be convenient moments in between in which one can get a prayer in, but it will not be ideal, liable to interruption at any moment. And so finally comes the return home, where at last one can relax and may be able to pray as one should really wish.

Not everybody's life is spent in this way, of course. People may be unemployed, or sick, or solitary or looking after young children. But what I am trying to say is that our prayers should not be like those said in the monastery or convent, even if we should like them to be.

Let us consider the teaching of St Teresa and St John of the Cross, for it is they, after all, who are the great cosmologists of the soul, and have left us the pattern of prayer as a means of knowing God. And here perhaps a word is due about knowing. What exactly does knowing God mean? We think we know all about him when we have read the gospels, listened to the Church's teaching, especially that which is contained in the creeds, and above all taken in the person of Jesus who said (John 14:9) 'He who has seen me has seen the Father.' But there is all the difference between knowing about a person and knowing him directly. Details in the former case may involve a search on the internet, gathering information from friends, or, particularly if they are dead, reading a biography. But the latter, intimate knowledge, can only be acquired by direct experience, by spending time with the person, by being with them face to face. This is what we call knowledge of a person; anyone who has experience of knowing a very dear person, more particularly God, will realise that knowing about him is a very poor substitute.

Although there are minor differences between them, what Teresa and John have to say about the spiritual life is essentially the same. Each teaches that the way to perfection is through prayer; and each divides the spiritual life into three phases which may broadly be termed the purgative, the illuminative, and the unitive. The first, which includes what John calls the dark night of the senses, is essentially active: that is to say, it is a period of purgation in which the soul is proceeding by its own efforts, and has not yet come to any direct knowledge of God. In the second, however, which Teresa (though she varies in her appellations) calls the Prayer of Quiet in *The Interior Castle*, a marked difference occurs. The soul gets to know God directly, more usually in short glimpses, and though it longs for these periods to be prolonged, it is torn between the joy of his presence and a longing, so intense that it amounts to a state of real suffering, for his return. We call these direct experiences of God contemplation, and John takes it for granted that all for whom he is writing will attain them. His concern is that they should not linger there, should not be so deceived by the pleasures they find there that they lose sight of the end for which they should be pressing. Teresa is more moderate: she acknowledges that not all souls will come to contemplation, and that those who do not are also capable of holiness. But in both saints the emphasis is on the mystical knowledge of God which can only be obtained by prayer.

St Thérèse of Lisieux was also a Carmelite, and might have been expected to embrace the same path, particularly as she had a great reverence for both the Spanish saints, and once said that at the age of seventeen and eighteen she had no other spiritual nourishment than St John. But the path she followed was entirely different, and amounts to a revolution in the way the spiritual life is approached. Her method of spirituality, which she described as direct and short and new, was designed to bring the soul to holiness through simple actions to which she gave the term 'little way'. It was essentially a way of total dedication to God, of offering up to him all that she did, and of finding him in small acts of charity, which she describes in her autobiographical documents, and which largely passed unnoticed during her life. It is far from being a passive state, though the term 'spiritual childhood' has often been applied to it, as if the soul had nothing to do of its own account but could rest serenely in the arms of Jesus. It was on the contrary a very active pursuit of charity, as is shown by the efforts it cost her, and by her statement that natural impulses run totally contrary to the teachings of Jesus.

By now it should be obvious what I am advocating. Though there is no doubting the holiness of Teresa and John of the Cross, and the truth of what they say in their exploration of the path to be travelled by the soul before it can fully know God, theirs is not the method of spirituality which best suits the lay person. For this we have to go to Thérèse of Lisieux and make her little way our own.

This, of course, is not to dismiss prayer, or to decry its importance in the spiritual life. Enough has been said in a previous chapter to show how vital it is. Through it we learn how we should conduct our lives and we ask for God's help in doing so. We express our penitence if we have sinned. We intercede on behalf of other people, including the dead. And we thank God for all that he has done for us. It is certain that he listens to our prayers and answers them, though not always in the way we should like. But we should not expect prayer to do for us what we can do for ourselves, though God is always there in the background. And above all we should recognise that it is not the method of sanctification which God has given to laypeople.

There exists, however, among the laity a class of people to whom what I have said does not apply. These are the natural contemplatives whose spiritual lives are very similar to what St Teresa and St John of the Cross have described. And of course, they should persevere in their prayer, and hope to meet God by these means. But they are likely to be few, and the bulk of this chapter is not aimed at them.

All this, however, leaves us with a problem. For nothing I have said so far suggests that lay folk can achieve the same degree of holiness as the conventual. We have either to return to the theory of the two classes, those who have, in the words of Jesus, chosen 'the better way' as compared with the vast majority of Christians who are destined to toil away without hope of spiritual reward on earth; or we have to recognise that the latter are just as capable of achieving union with God as their conventual counterparts.

I have already hinted at a solution to this problem by saying how accurately Teresa and John have mapped out the stages through which the soul must pass in its journey to God. This path is incumbent on all, lay or religious. In other words, people will differ greatly in the way they experience God on earth, but the journey that they must travel remains the same. We each have to purge ourselves by our own efforts, and then suffer the passive purgation to which John of the Cross gives the name 'dark night of the spirit'.

The active, or purgative, stage is easy to understand. We all of us recognise that we have faults that need to be cleansed if we are to make any progress in our journey towards God (this is why, incidentally, Teresa lays such emphasis on self-examination, for it is only if we dig deep down, if we are totally honest with ourselves over our faults, that we can hope to be rid of them). But the illuminative stage is much harder to explain. Certain people, it appears, encounter God on earth and experience great joy through it. But most of us, if we were asked, would deny that we enjoy such privileges. So we are, it appears yet again, in an inferior position.

The dilemma, however, can be resolved if we consider contemplation as just one part of the soul's journey on earth. It is given to some people to encourage them on that journey, to make them aware that they have chosen the right path, and, in certain cases, so that they can pass on their knowledge to others. But it still amounts to only a stage on that journey, and we should look in the lives of lay people for its equivalent elsewhere.

I believe that this equivalent will be expressed in the way they experience the spiritual life. In fact, rather than meet God directly, which will totally change all that they have known before, their version of what would be contemplation for one in a cloistered community is likely to consist of a new joy in the performance of their religious activities: fear will vanish, or be largely diminished. Where before they might have been behaving out of compulsion, performing from a strong sense of duty, they will now find themselves able to act much more naturally, as if the impulse of their lives changed from duty to something much closer to the love of God which they had always hoped to find. They may not wish to analyse too deeply the new joy they experience, but they will almost certainly realise that it is not something which they could have come to on their own and must therefore be associated with God. And provided they do not slacken in their efforts to serve God, this new-found freedom will remain with them.

Thus their joy will be of a different kind from that which the contemplative feels. They may not have the direct experience of God which is given to the latter, but what they do have will have an immediate effect on the way they go about their Christian lives. There will be a lightening of the will for a start. The demands of the Christian life will not be less, but these will no longer seem to require such an effort. Conforming to the law of God and performing certain deeds of charity which in the past seemed to go totally against the grain will gradually become easier and pleasanter. This, I believe, is the equivalent for the layperson of the direct knowledge of God for the contemplative. We cannot tell how many Christians reach this stage, but it is certainly available to all who treat the call to charity as assiduously as those in the cloister apply themselves to prayer.

But why, it may be asked, does God make this distinction? Why does he not grant to lay people the same gifts which, we are told, are granted to those in the cloister? There is a fairly simple explanation for this, and it is that he does not want to distract us from our earthly duties. In other words, if he were to make contemplatives of all of us, if we were to be constantly on the lookout for the next spiritual experience, it is likely that we should turn inwards, and should neglect the world in which he wishes us to make our lives. And by this God shows us how much he values every aspect of his creation, not simply that which is directly connected with Christianity. We still tend to think of certain occupations as having something more religious about them: the nurse, for instance, the teacher, the foster-carer. And it is true that these occupations give us better opportunities to love God and to respect the call for charity than, say, does the life of a large company director or a financier. But this does not mean that God does not love the latter as much as the former, or that he is not concerned that all, and not simply those whom we value the more, should find their eventual place in heaven. Nor does it mean that he does not wish that the whole of society, secular as well as religious, should function as ably as it might. At one time the two were thought to be in direct opposition to each other, or at least that God was concerned only with safeguarding the latter. Now, fortunately, this distinction is no longer made. We recognise that he is involved in every corner of our society, that the only thing, in fact, which does not reflect his will is sin.

John and Teresa say that the illuminative life lasts a long time, twenty years or more, and we should not be surprised if the same applies to what I have said of laypeople, all the time growing closer to God and learning to serve him better. But eventually there comes a time when even this is not enough, when we pass through a stage in which our previous joy, our previous sense of being well in God's favour evaporates, and we are left in total darkness. This is what John calls 'the dark night of the spirit', and it is applicable to all souls, contemplative or not, though, like the illuminative stage, it may be perceived in different ways. It is a state of passive cleansing: God is so different from his creation that something special is needed before we can fully get to know him. John and others have used the analogy of a candle and the sun. So long as we are in a dimly lighted sphere, a candle is sufficient for our needs. But the closer we come to the sun, in this case God, the more useless a candle becomes.

But there is another way of thinking of the dark night of the spirit, and this is that even after all our efforts to purge ourselves, something remains, and it is probably equivalent to the legacy of original sin, which comes between us and God. Before this is dealt with, we are incapable of being admitted to his presence. And only he can provide the remedy. It is as if we could only look so far into ourselves, and for a full knowledge of what we are, someone who can see us from the outside, someone who stands apart from us, is required. John writes extensively of this state: indeed, one of his books is called *The Dark Night of the Soul.* He may, as Ruth Burrows says, exaggerate its horrors, but there is no doubting the word of those who have suffered from it, including Teresa, who largely agrees with him, that it is a very hard trial indeed, equivalent to purgatory in which the soul is totally passive, and that during this time the very hope of salvation may disappear.

But since I have said that all souls must pass through it, how does it affect the layperson? I believe that the 'dark night of the spirit' will involve for them events in the real world in the same way that contemplation was for them linked to what they closely knew. In other words, they will not suffer to the same extent the spiritual pangs of which St John writes, though they may well feel deserted by God; but they will be subjected to real tests of endurance, such as abound in our earthly existence, namely severe illness, bereavement, or a period of unemployment. This is not to say that God brings such things upon us, but that he takes advantage of them in order to complete his process of purgation.

How, then, are we to conduct ourselves during this state? John of the Cross makes much use of the word faith during this time, and it is true that it is the only weapon we have. But it is faith in the sense of endurance, quite unlike anything we have known before. Just as the equivalent state of contemplation was passed in the world which lay people well knew, so this new one is strongly tied to the outside world. They may well lose all sense of God during this time, find prayer hard, if not impossible, but they are still called upon to endure, to behave as if belief were there, to continue the efforts at charity and all that is involved in the spiritual life which have previously been their life's work.

But another question arises. How, if this involves the natural accidents to which life is prone – the illnesses, the bereavements, the sudden shocks – may this state be identified as a spiritual one, rather than one which just occurs naturally? Well, one answer will be that it is only likely to be perceived as such by those who have persevered in the spiritual life. But the other answer is that it does not matter. For both believers and non-believers there is only one remedy, to endure (though Teresa says that one should not be so overwhelmed by this state that one neglects the little diversions which can make it easier). And in any case it may be better not to know, for there is nothing worse in the spiritual life than constantly looking back, constantly trying to diagnose where one is on the spiritual ladder.

Eventually – and it seems probable that about two to three years is the norm – the darkness lightens, and the joy which one had always associated with the spiritual life returns, but much enhanced. This is not to say that the outward sufferings to which one has been subject will clear. Nothing, after all, can reverse bereavement, and an illness can remain just as troubling as it once was. But now there is nothing more to be feared, nothing more to be desired, except the final consummation with God in heaven, which some have longed for. But the desire to die, and thus be wholly with him, is much less likely to be felt by the layperson than by one who has got to this point by prayer. For the former is still firmly anchored in the world, and there is plenty to enjoy there, plenty to absorb one's interest. This is the beginning of the end, for it leads to total union with God, which is what the soul longs for and for which it was made.

CONSCIENCE AND SIN

Is conscience always a reliable guide to human behaviour? It is the best guide we have, but we should realise that it is not always fully informed, and is also very easily liable to manipulation.

It also seems to vary from individual to individual; which is not to say that there are not universal moral laws that conscience obliges one to obey. But the way in which we judge failure to observe such laws certainly varies.

Take, for instance, the case of stealing. Stealing, we know, is wrong, but what are we to make of the individual who steals a loaf of bread knowing that without it he or she, not to mention their children, will starve? Are they to be judged by the same criteria by which we judge a person who cold-bloodedly falsifies accounts and steals from his employer? In the Nazi concentration camps the normal laws of acceptable human behaviour seem to have totally broken down. Thus Roman Frister (*The Cap*) describes how finding that his cap, without which he was sure to be executed at the morning parade, was missing, he stole that of a fellow prisoner and thus ensured his own survival and the latter's death. On the other hand Maximilian Kolbe volunteered to take the place of a prisoner condemned to death for attempting to escape, and himself was put to death by starvation. Likewise, during the Nazi occupation some, at great danger to themselves, sheltered the Jews, whereas others, if they did not actually denounce them, turned a blind eye to what was going on and simply did their best to survive. Still others took advantage of a situation which gave them boundless opportunities on the black market. We are indeed fortunate that in this country we were never faced with such choices.

Or, a final example, I am writing this in the midst of the Brexit controversy. Some MPs are doubtless aware of their constituents' wishes, and are subordinating their own conviction of what best serves the country to those. But we may assume that the vast majority are acting according to what their conscience tells them. How comes it, then, unless conscience acts in different ways in different people, that the House is hopelessly divided, and that no solution has been found?

Since, however, this book is mainly about Christianity, we had better confine ourselves to the notion of sin, and how it affects the individual. Or rather not simply the individual, but the community as a whole, for the Church has become much more aware during the last few years of how a single act, whether for good or evil, may have enormous repercussions on the community as a whole. And in this it somewhat resembles chaos theory, which holds that the single fluttering of a butterfly's wings may set off a chain of events which results in a hurricane at the other end.

The early Church seems to have been much more aware of this phenomenon than we have become in recent times. It was very community based. Thus St Paul, writing to the Corinthians, tells them that a single sin, in this case a man living with his father's wife, blackens them all, and that the only remedy is to expel him from the community. Sinners had to acknowledge their sin publicly, they had to stand aside from the community, and wait for a considerable period of time until they were readmitted to full church membership in a ceremony presided over by a bishop. Compare that to what is the practice now, and what was the practice until a few years ago when it was just a question of personal guilt, as opposed to an offence against the community. But though the outward appurtenances of the ceremony may have changed, still all the offender has to do is confess his sins privately to a priest; though one hopes it is made clear to him, and that he himself realises, that it is not just a personal matter, but something that affects the well-being of the whole Church.

Another thing that has changed in our time is the awareness of our duty to take care of our planet, and how much we have neglected this duty in the past when, for instance, there seemed nothing wrong with the slaughter of wild animals, now considered at risk, and when coal was apparently an endless resource which one could use at will without thinking of the harm it might do. Pope Francis' encyclical *Laudato Si'* has been of enormous help in emphasising this need, which is one more way of evading the individualism associated with the confession of sin. I am not suggesting we should go to confession every time we flush a baby wipe down the toilet, or leave the car with its engine running, but certainly an ecological outlook is something which we should all cultivate, and which unites us with those outside the Church who also have this on their minds.

But perhaps we should at this moment define sin. It is an offence against God. It is worth here quoting Newman's comment on sin: 'She [the Catholic Church] holds that it were better....for all the many millions who are upon it [the earth] to die of starvation in extremest agony, as far as temporal affliction goes, than that one soul, I will not say should be lost, but should commit one single venial sin.'* This is unattractive, and seems to ignore the part played by God's mercy, but it does bring out the enormity of sin. It is something utterly alien to God's nature, something far removed from anything we can conceive of him.

Catholic theology divides sins into two kinds, venial and mortal (though the term is not much heard these days. Preachers prefer to talk of 'serious' sins, though the term 'mortal' is still mentioned in the Catholic catechism).

Venial sins – from the Latin 'venia', pardon – are not so serious as mortal. They are not capable of cutting off the soul entirely from God, and they do not have to be confessed to a priest, though the catechism is in favour of doing so. Mortal sins – from the Latin 'mors', death – are what the word suggests. They are fatal, capable of sending the soul to hell if unrepented. Luckily the catechism is careful in its definition of mortal sin: it has to be sin whose object is 'grave matter [that is to say, sin against one of the Ten Commandments] and which is also committed with full knowledge and deliberate consent.'

When I first became a Catholic, in 1957, failure to attend Mass on Sunday was certainly talked about as a mortal sin, so I wondered about the condition of a person who had fulfilled the law of God in every way, who had excelled in charity, but who had decided one Sunday morning, without any saving excuse, to miss Mass. Would he automatically go to hell? It was a totally theoretical speculation, for neither of the conditions applied to me: I was neither perfect, and nor was I in danger of missing Mass. But it did seem to me at least to put a limitation on God's mercy, to have a mistaken view of what sin was about.

Since then there have been other changes in the official view of sin. Masturbation, for instance, which I am fairly convinced was regarded as a mortal sin, and to which I confessed with unfailing regularity, is now classed simply as 'an intrinsically and gravely disordered action', which still seems a bit excessive where such a common fault is concerned, though various let-outs are mentioned, such as the force of acquired habit and psychological or social factors. The same terminology, 'intrinsically disordered', is applied to homosexual acts, though fortunately not to the homosexual inclination, since science seems to show that our sexual orientation is born within us, and to condemn it would therefore be to condemn something which, for his own purposes, God has created. But this still leaves homosexuals in a bind, which the catechism itself acknowledges, for it seems that they must live their lives in a state of total chastity if they are to achieve perfection. I myself believe that the Church will in time find itself able to confer a blessing on those of the same sex who choose to live together in a non-sexual partnership – one cannot call this marriage, for this is confined to union between a man and a woman – but even so, this does not limit the disadvantages under which homosexuals are bound to suffer compared to others. So it may well be that 'the virtues of self-mastery', which is what the catechism recommends, are the best that can be offered them.

Mortal sin, as I say, has to be confessed to a priest as soon as possible, since it totally cuts the soul off from God. But it is not simply a matter of looking through a book and deciding whether or not one has committed such and such a sin. For one thing, another change that has come over the Catholic church in the last few years is the emphasis on the fact that sin consists as much of the things that one has failed to do as those which one has done, and so runs the formula which is repeated at the start of every Mass. Ideally conscience should tell one when one has committed a mortal sin, but this is not always the case. Some people have a tender conscience which becomes instantly aware, from a change in their innermost being, when they have committed a sin which sets them apart from God, while others with less sensitive consciences may scarcely be aware that they have done something which puts them in need of urgent confession. (It is worth here, incidentally, once again turning to science, which has shown that psychopaths have no sense of right and wrong – in other words lack a conscience – while there is a certain type of criminal in whom, whether from birth or from what he has already gone through, the part of the brain which distinguishes right from wrong is seriously diminished. All this should preclude one from making moral judgements too hastily.)

I come now to abortion, which is rightly regarded as a grave sin by the Catholic church, since it involves the killing of a potential human being. But here again conscience has to be considered, since millions of women disagree with this view and would not regard abortion as a sin at all. They may be reluctant to undergo it, and may feel bad about it afterwards, but they still view it as a 'woman's right to choose' (another slogan, 'a woman's right to control her own body', seems to me less well chosen, since it totally ignores the fact that that same body is carrying an embryo within it).

Pope Francis has recently downgraded abortion as a sin which, like desecration of the Eucharist and breaking the seal of the confessional, came into a special category for which absolution had to be sought from a bishop. It is now classed in the list of 'ordinary' mortal sins, one which can be mentioned during a routine confession, and which can be pardoned by a priest. And this is surely right, since there was a danger, particularly in America, that a Catholic was defined solely by his stand over abortion.

But there is another issue where conscience is most strongly involved, and this concerns rape, and particularly rape of a minor. What is one to think of the recent case of a thirteen-year-old, raped by a member of her family, and compelled to go through with childbirth all because a high-up member of the church decreed it and threatened with excommunication anyone who helped her obtain an abortion? This is surely a case where mercy should override church law. But the whole issue of rape in general, not simply rape of a minor, is one that deserves further consideration. Catholic theology teaches that sex has two functions, unitive and reproductive, and that the two are closely related. Anything therefore that artificially comes between the desire to have sex and its natural consequence is to be condemned. But where rape is concerned, the unitive part of the action is certainly absent. The woman has not given consent to the way her body is being used. Should she therefore be compelled to go through with the reproductive part, to give birth to a child when the unitive side of the act, the voluntary coming together, is missing?

Compassion at least suggests that this is another area where rigid adherence to church law, in this case, the sanctity of any human life, however small, runs up against the purpose for which sex was created. There is a good case for saying that mercy overrides law in such circumstances, rather as it does in the case of divorced but remarried Catholics who were banned from receiving Communion so long as they were in a sexual relationship with their partner. Pope Francis has recently put this in the hands of bishops – in other words restored the principle of the 'internal forum' which was in operation before Pope St John Paul II put a stop to it; and there is a case for saying that abortion, where rape is concerned, should be treated in the same way.

So what are the sins that one ought to confess? Until comparatively recently – and I have given an illustration of that fact – sexual sins ranked very high in the list of such offences, almost as if nothing else were capable of blackening one in the sight of God. And it is true that the Church has been slow to come to terms with sexuality, to see the good in it, as well as the evil uses to which it can be put. But when Jesus is explaining to his disciples that what goes into the mouth is blameless compared to what comes out of it and proceeds from the heart, sexual offences are only part of a list which includes such spiritual sins as evil thoughts, false witness and slander. And there are plenty of other things he might have mentioned: envy, jealousy, anger, even lust which dominates our thoughts but is not released in action. These are the spiritual sins which deface us more than any other. Yes, sleeping with one's boy/girlfriend before marriage is wrong, though it has become an almost universal practice, and recent polls have shown that even Catholics no longer regard it as a sin (which is a sign of how far the way in which society thinks has penetrated their own thought). However, it is worth remembering that there is often real love involved in such unions, and they seem dwarfed by the spiritual sins I have already mentioned.

But it has to be said that confession is a bit the luck of the draw: in other words, one may come across a wise priest, ready to tell one what is really wrong with one's soul; or one may light upon one who lays an undue emphasis on the sins of the flesh and for whom everything else takes second place.

I have already mentioned the fact that conscience is liable to manipulation. We all know the symptoms even if we have not yielded to them: I'll just do it this once and never again; everybody does it and so why shouldn't I; it's a victimless crime, isn't it? So how does this affect the question of sin? It is tempting to think that one can make up for a lifetime of misdeeds by a deathbed repentance. Graham Greene was very fond of playing with this idea, quoting, in one of his novels, the 17th century couplet:

> Between the stirrup and the ground
> He mercy sought and mercy found.

But sins have a way of turning into habits, and habits can become so ingrained that they are hard to break. It seems possible that this is what Jesus meant about the 'sin against the Holy Ghost', which he says, unlike any other, will never be forgiven. It is rare to find Jesus talking in this way. But is the gist of what he is saying that the consequence of a lifetime of accumulated sin is that at the end, one is incapable of feeling the need for pardon, let alone asking for it? In other words, as well as being an offence against God and the community, sin is certainly something which has repercussions on oneself.

It is sometimes thought that after death one passes before God as before a tribunal, and that he either raises his thumb or puts it down to decide one's fate. But isn't it likely that the damned, if such there be, are not so much being judged by God as having judged themselves? They have put themselves out of the reach of God by killing within themselves anything that partakes of his nature. Thus they have nothing in common with him when they die, and their fate is sealed, not by any outside tribunal, but by what they have made of themselves.

As well as personal sin, there is also original sin to deal with: something which secularists are inclined to deny, but whose effects can everywhere be seen. This is because we are naturally ingrained to put our own wills ahead of that of God. Saint Paul has given a vivid description of this state when he says, in Romans 7:21-5:

> So I find it to be a law that when I want to do right, evil lies close at hand. For I delight in the law of God, in my inmost self, but I see in my members another law at war with the law of my mind and making me captive to the law of sin which dwells in my members. Wretched man that I am! Who will deliver me from this body of death? Thanks be to God through Jesus Christ our Lord! So then, I of myself serve the law of God with my mind, but with my flesh [by which he means the natural, unredeemed man] I serve the law of sin.

Nobody knows how original sin came into the world. So long as the story of Adam and Eve was literally believed in, it was fairly easy to account for. Adam was the first man, and yielding to his wife Eve – which incidentally gave a perfect excuse for blackening her and her sex – who was herself tempted by the serpent, he brought sin into the world. Nowadays, however, the Genesis story is seen as but one attempt to explain the presence of evil in the world, and the situation becomes more complicated. For instance, who was this man who sinned against God, setting himself above his creator, and how and why was this sin passed on to the rest of creation? The Catholic catechism explains this by saying that Adam, or the first man to sin, is representative of humanity, and that this explains why the sin is passed on from generation to generation, but adds that we must be content to leave the 'how' as a mystery. This has not stopped theologians throughout the ages trying to resolve the question, notably Augustine, who taught that the result of original sin was 'concupiscence', a rather unfortunate word, since it implies, but in this case does not mean, sexual desire, so much as a tendency to prefer one's own ends over those of

God, and that it is transmitted through the normal process of generation.

However, disregarding the fact that the whole thing is shrouded in mystery, natural curiosity emboldens one to ask a further question. Whoever was guilty of this first sin – and the catechism affirms, in accordance with scripture, that it was committed by a real person, one of our ancestors – must have lived a long time ago, when worship, such as it was, would have been directed towards the things of nature, the sun, the moon, stars, and so on. It requires a certain degree of sophistication or intelligence to rebel against God. Would primitive man have been capable of it? But perhaps we should follow the recommendations of the catechism, abandon such speculation, and concentrate instead on the consequences of the Fall.

Baptism, through the benefits which Jesus won for the human race, erases the guilt of original sin, but still leaves one with its consequences: the proneness to seek one's own will in preference to that of God. The Easter feast begins with the notion of 'felix culpa', the idea that had it not been for Adam's sin, grace, in the form of Jesus' entry into the world and his redemptive power, would never have occurred either. To that extent, therefore, we should be grateful to Adam and Eve. But there is a further reason for regarding them with gratitude. We do not know, of course, whether they would have remained in the garden content with their simple pastoral life had sin never occurred. Would they have had children? There is no indication of this. All we know is that, once they had sinned, they became aware of their nakedness, and from that point on sex became associated with shame.

But there is another reason for regarding them with gratitude. When they were expelled from the garden human life changed. They were forced to live in the world as we know it, a world marred by hatreds, war, starvation and disease. But these were not the only things that were the consequence of their life outside the garden. Human beings have been forced to counter their propensity to sin with their instinct for creativity. We have Adam and Eve, and their life outside the garden, to thank for such wonders as Chartres Cathedral, the St Matthew Passion, the works of Dante and Shakespeare, as well as the whole process of scientific discovery, led, perhaps, by the very same curiosity which drove Eve to taste the apple. These, as well as the evils we daily see, are the consequences of the Fall, and we should never stop giving thanks to God for them, as well as for the gift of his Son.

Note

*It is worth contrasting Newman's view of sin with that of Julian of Norwich, when she says that 'Sin is behovely'. She does not mean by this that it is good or fitting to sin – compare, for instance, her saying with that of St Paul in Romans 6:1, where he utterly rejects the idea that one should remain in sin so that grace should abound. What she means is that it is inevitable that sin will come, but that God has contrived to find means to deal with it. I know which of the statements I find more comforting, and who I would rather have at my deathbed.

Lightning Source UK Ltd.
Milton Keynes UK
UKHW040659050921
389934UK00001B/87